D0863006

Forging a Nation

The Story of Mexico
From the Aztecs to the Present

Kathryn S. Blair

San Miguel Historical Press   Mexico City, Mexico

Copyright © 2011 by Kathryn S. Blair

This edition was prepared for printing by
Ghost River Images
5350 East Fourth Street
Tucson, Arizona 85711
www.ghostriverimages.com

To contact the author or order more copies of this book
forginganation.com

ISBN 978-1-4663-3747-3

Library of Congress Control Number: 2011911032

Printed in the United States of America
September, 2011
10 9 8 7 6 5 4 3 2 1

Contents

Dedication
To my dearly loved family
who live on both sides of the border.

INTRODUCTION

I have lived in Mexico for seventy years. Mexico has always been my home, my base. Born in Cuba, I arrived in Mexico with my American parents when I was three. My husband is Mexican and we have children, grandchildren and great- grandchildren on both sides of the border.

I grew up in two Mexicos: the warm, Latin culture in which "time" is measured by what is important at the moment, priorities change and one adjusts to the circumstances. The other was the Anglo-Saxon world of rules and planning ahead.

As a child I was drawn to the magic remedies of the herb woman, the scent of candle wax in a dark church, street performers, the irresistible smell of a taco sizzling on a street corner and the lilting music of a marimba. If I lost something I could turn Saint Anthony upside down in the house of my best Mexican friend and I would find it. You intoned a special prayer and his magical power made lost objects appear (Saint Anthony didn´t care if you were Episcopalian). The American School was a cross-ethnic babble of accents since the embassies sent children of every religion and color to learn English.

Pausing to peer in a store window or watch an organ grinder´s monkey do his tricks seemed more important than running to be on time. Being late did not require an apology. In Mexico, many days simply unfolded without the restrictions of a set program. Spontaneous response to the circumstance moved the day.

My Anglo-Saxon Mexico was summed up in the frustrating comments made by my father and his American friends who shared our table. "Why can´t they do things right? They agree to something and then do as they please." Favorite topics were the infamous graft, the mañana mentality, and the lack of maintenance. "But give a Mexican a wire and he can fix anything," my father also commented with admiration. If Mexicans were guests we heard loud complaints and criticisms of the government, but a spontaneous joke broke up the argument and a shrug of the shoulders meant "*Asi es, let's get on to something else*".

For many of my transient American friends, "the Mexican connection" left an indelible mark, an unexplainable nostalgia buried in the heart. No matter how many times my father claimed that "God's country is north of the Rio Grande." He never left. He died in Mexico at the age of ninety-seven.

As a lifetime observer and participant in things Mexican, I am ever fascinated with the ability of Mexicans to adjust to circumstance. As a student of Mexican history I marvel at the infinite conflicts it has survived. Mexico is ancient yet still emerging, trying to define itself. Like the outer walls of the great temple in the ancient Aztec Capital, Mexico has grown layer upon layer. Nothing seems to ever be finished – permanent. With a population of approximately twenty million, Mexico City is constantly in a state of "replanning". Streets that go one way today may go the other way tomorrow.

To many foreigners, Mexico presents contrasts difficult to understand: extreme wealth and grinding poverty, skyscrapers and huts, a bright, well educated, well traveled class and illiterate, hungry peasants.

Today fifty-three or more indigenous languages and dialects still survive but the pure, indigenous population is gradually facing extinction. The Conquest forged a new class of Mexicans- *the mestizo,* a mixture of varying degrees of Spanish and indigenous cultures and skin tones. After Independence, a small remnant of American and European investors remained in Mexico and added to the mix, and since then, people from around the world have become Mexicans. About one hundred and ten million people comprise the population. They speak a common language, Spanish, and most share a common religion, Catholic. But they do not share the wealth. The thin layer at the top are the very wealthy. Carlos Slim, the richest man in the world (according to Forbes 400) is a Mexican. The thick layer below the rich comprises the emerging upper and lower middle classes. Below them fifty percent of the population is underpaid, poorly educated (some not at all) rural and urban classes struggling to feed their families. For both the highly trained professionals and poverty stricken lower class, the view across the border looks like Valhalla.

About twelve million legal and illegal Mexicans are living in the United States today. These immigrants have added a new spice to the American "Melting Pot" – *Chile.* Now, in any U.S. supermarket one can find Mexican food. Mexican restaurants abound. Unlike the early European immigrants who created the "Melting Pot", most Mexicans have retained their culture and language. They have only to step back across the border to revitalize those ties. Radio stations blare out Mexican music and *telenovelas* are broadcast in Spanish. In cities like Los Angeles and San Antonio one hears as much Spanish as English. Many book stores carry books in Spanish and Spanish words are seeping into the English language.

For generations Americans fixed their sights across the Atlantic ocean; they ignored the Rio Grande. Now, they have discovered that the Rio Grande is only a narrow river and that Mexicans know how to swim. Heated debates have been ongoing in Congress concerning what to do about these immigrants who keep pouring over the border. The problems of immigration are multiple. Compounded by the drug traffic, today it has become a giant headache for both Mexico and the United States. The biggest drug market in the world lies north of the border and proximity to that market has Mexico in a bind.

When I was fifteen, I was sent to the United States to finish high school. I quickly found out what culture shock meant. To Americans, Mexico was the border towns – dirt roads, mangy dogs, half naked children. They could not believe that *My* Mexico was a city of volcanoes and pyramids, an opera house, a castle, beautiful gardens and classmates from all over the world. I vowed that some day

I would help to correct this ignorance.

Knowing the history of a country helps to understand its people. It is in this context that I have written my "story" of Mexico.

Kathryn Skidmore Blair

Mexico City 2011

Other books by Kathryn Blair

In The Shadow Of The Angel
(intheshadowoftheangel.com)

PROLOGUE

There is a two thousand mile border between Mexico and the United States, and beneath that border there is a five thousand year history. The Spanish conquered Mexico one hundred years before the pilgrims landed in Massachusetts. For the most part, nomadic Indians roamed the northern part of America, but before the Conquest, indigenous empires had been built and vanished in Mexico.

Who are these many-faceted Mexicans? Masks and sculptures of their ancient past show Asian, Negro, Semitic, even Caucasian features. All mysterious beginnings. Mesoamerican culture still baffles archeologists and anthropologists. One thing we do know: Mexico, the current nation, was born of fire and fused in three hundred years of Spanish rule. From the Conquest in 1521, indigenous Mexico was pounded and molded into a nation, wobbling to its feet as a nation of mixed races when Independence was won in 1821. After a century of bitter conflicts, power struggles, the invasion of its territory by the United States and later France, civil war, a long dictatorship and a devastating Revolution, stability finally began to take root in the 1920s. Today, Mexico is a dynamic, youthful nation, governed by its own brand of democracy.

The history of Mexico is a chronicle of on-going transformation. As the new millennium began, Mexico shifted once again. The elections of July 2, 2000, in which Vicente Fox, an opposition candidate, won, broke the base of the one-party system (PRI) which had governed the country for seventy-one years. Today, Mexico is living a transcendental period, a period of transition from total authoritarian rule to a wobbly democracy. The word "dialogue" is inching its way into government The North American Free Trade Agreement, signed by Canada, the United States and Mexico, engendered new commercial enterprises. The money immigrants send home is a major contribution to the Mexican economy and the work of immigrants in the United States is contributing to the U.S. economy. One hopes that this growing interdependence will bring a better appreciation and understanding of the differences and problems on each side of the border. Communities on both sides of the border are now joining to seek solutions to common problems.

Peeling off the layers of the past has been an intriguing task. History is made by people and is not bound by geographic perimeters. Events that happen in one place may rebound to affect another place on earth. In this context I invite you to go beyond the linear record of dates and facts and savor the magic which makes Mexico unique.

CHAPTER I

Since earth was created, mysterious forces have churned within her nucleus and she has been affected by cosmic phenomena. When man first stood erect, he looked up with awe and wonder. He has been in awe of that gigantic celestial canopy ever since. The indigenous people of Mexico looked always upward, to the heavens. It was the home of the Gods who ruled the elements to which they were subject and upon which their existence depended. The sixteenth century Spaniard focused his attention on the ground, looking for material answers. His God had walked upon the earth.

THE SETTING

From the tip of South America the mighty mountain chain of the Andes rims the Pacific coast running northward from snow-covered heights to the equator. At the Isthmus of Panama it descends to the sea, then snakes upward through Central America and rises again to snow-covered peaks in Mexico. Here the northern continent begins to widen and this prodigious mountain range separates into two branches, the western and eastern Sierra Madre, creating an extensive high plateau at their juncture.

Cutting their jagged, twin routes through Mexico these towering ranges divide the country into isolated regions, separate and distinct. Predisposed by their geographic positions, more than 160 different languages and cultures were rooted. Cloud-shrouded heights and tropical jungles exist on the same parallel, the same mountain in Mexico. Vertical cornfields seem to defy the law of gravity.

Arid north, verdant south, mountains precipitously falling off to long, tropical beaches. Violent storms lash the Gulf of Mexico while warm breezes graze the Pacific side. Hidden valleys are sheltered by mountains, deep ravines and canyons between. A few small lakes, fewer rivers, none navigable for long distances. Naked, sterile soil in high, flat areas is swept by dust storms and flash floods, wastelands left by belching volcanoes. There, only cactus and spiny thickets abound. Across a gorge, a stream feeds an exuberant valley. Precious water is scarce. Thick pine forests cover one side of a mountain, eroded slopes the other. A mosaic of altitudes, vegetation and climates is this parcel of the planet known as Mexico.

THE FIRST SETTLERS

About seven thousand years ago, nomadic hunter-gatherers circulated throughout Mexico. In 3000 B.C. they began to settle in villages. The first to leave important evidence of their existence in Mesoamerica was an unknown people called the *Olmeca*. In 1200 B.C. the *Olmeca* settled in the forested lowlands along the Gulf coast of Mexico where the northern continent funnels down to a narrow waist. Their religion was grounded in the natural and cosmic worlds and the powerful Jaguar was their God. The *Olmeca* created great ceremonial centers, devised a calendar and dug irrigation canals, pushing on in 500 B.C. to leave traces of their culture as far north as the valley of *Anahuac*, site of Mexico City today. In the southern state of Tabasco, they left giant stone heads in the jungle to baffle future archeologists. Carved in basalt, as high as nine feet, these heads portray odd characteristics: helmets, thick lips, broad nostrils and slant eyes. Where the *Olmeca* came from is still being debated.

Below Tabasco, in the southernmost region of Mexico, a large peninsula juts out: Yucatán. Around the hump, the Caribbean sea is still and clear. Soft, turquoise waves brush white beaches and rain forests roof the adjoining jungle that ever covers mans´ traces. Here, the great *Maya* civilization flourished and collapsed. There are traces of settlers in lush valleys as early as 2000 B.C. But it was in the Classic Period of pre-Columbian history, between A.D.250-900, that this extraordinary civilization developed and reached its zenith. Spread over an extensive area, a diversity of geography, vegetation and mineral resources established a reciprocal need for the *Maya* people to trade. A complex of city-states was linked, their stone temples soaring above the jungle canopy. White, sand-covered roads wove through Mesoamerica, connecting cities that spanned Yucatán, Quintana Roo and Chiapas in Mexico, all of Guatemala and parts of El Salvador, Honduras and Belice in Central

America. The Lords of these city-states claimed dynastic heredity through lineage to the gods. Highly skilled as architects and astronomers, the *Maya* developed a calendar as accurate as the Gregorian. Their use of zero in their calculations predates the Hindu. Zero is nothing from which everything starts. Religion, art, politics and war wove the life patterns of the *Maya*. They read the future by observing cosmic cycles: crops sprouted, grew and died as seasons repeated themselves over and over, each feeding another cycle, like birth and death. Man is born of the earth but aspires to heaven. His transit here, they believed, is to throw light on the mystery of existence. Like the ancient Egyptians, the *Maya* developed a complex picture-writing system. History must be preserved to predict the future. And to understand his destiny, they believed man must look to the cosmos. There, the future was written.

As migrant tribes settled and prospered in the highlands of Mexico, the jungle encroached on the Classic Mayan civilization whose collapse has still not been satisfactorily explained.

Toward the beginning of the first millennium A.D., in the high central plateau, new agricultural, social and religious centers began to dominate the region. In this Classic Period the vast metropolis of *Teotihuacán* flourished and fell. Master builders, two great pyramids dedicated to the Sun and the Moon dominated its eight square-mile ceremonial center. In Oaxac*a, Mixteco* and *Zapotec* farmers were using irrigation agriculture and tracking celestial movements. As the millennium drew to a close, the most advanced highland civilization, the *Tolteca*, also declined and fell.

During roughly 3000 years divergent cultures left magnificent structures from the heights of the central valleys to the tropics in Mexico: *La Venta* in the State of Tabasco, *Teotihuacán* and *Tula* near Mexico City, *Monte Albán* and *Mitla* in the State of Oaxaca, *Palenque, Uxmal, Chichen Itza,* and *Tulum* in southern Mexico to mention some major sites. But more important, they left deep roots in the Mexican psyche.

Who were these people? How did they arrive? Many scholars have speculated: they were Asiatic tribes that came over the top of the world via the Bering Straits and migrated during thousands of years to warmer climates. Thor Hyerdahl suggests that the Gulf settlers arrived in reed boats from North Africa. Were the Maya the lost tribe of Israel? Did some cross the Pacific from India and China? One thing we do know: these clans, tribes and "Empires" created their own world, by themselves and of themselves. Until the Spanish Conquest they knew no other world.

THE VALLEY OF ANAHUAC

A land of harsh geography, altitude counts more than latitude in Mexico: cold country is up, hot country is down. Through the vast extension of the Republic, one place is privileged by nature above all others: the high central plateau, a great tableland thrust up with volcanic vigor millenniums ago when the Sierra Madre separated into its two ranges. Like a giant horseshoe, the valley of *Anahuac* crowns the long, central plateau. Two snow-capped volcanoes grace the panorama cutting a sharp silhouette against the once crystal transparency of an intense blue sky. Then, five interlocking shallow lakes mirrored the sheltering mountains that rose from the valley floor. Daylight faded quickly as the sun streaked the sky in a burst of glory and disappeared.

The valley of *Anahuac,* today is called the Valley of Mexico. Dry winter and dry spring turn a green landscape to brown, then luminous clouds again billow overhead and a long rainy season nourishes the parched earth where Mexico City is located. It was here, on an island, that the Aztecs founded their temple city, *Tenochtitlán*, in 1325 A.D. At an elevation of 7500 feet, the climate was dry and temperate. The rarefied air refracted a dazzling light. When Cortés conquered the Aztecs in 1521, *Tenochtitlán* was a breathtaking sight of temples, canals and causeways. But by the time Independence was won, 300 years later, the lakes had virtually disappeared, drained or filled in by the Spaniards as the baroque Capital of New Spain was superimposed on the ruins of brightly colored geometric structures.

Anahuac: site of ancient empires, of the powerful seat of New Spain, site of the Capital of the Republic of Mexico. Today, Mexico City sprawls in every direction, often obscuring the mountains with smog and clogging new through- ways with traffic. Hot in the sun. Cool in the shade. Warm days. Chilly nights. Bright daylight. Dark shadows. The changing light blends the seen and unseen in the Valley of Mexico creating a different reality.

ADVENT OF THE AZTECS[1]

In about 1260 A.D. a ragged tribe of wanderers, known as *Mexicas*[1] were searching for a place to settle in the central highland of Mexico. For nearly two centuries they had wandered, landless, friendless and persecuted, guided by their Priest-Astrologer, *Tenoch*. The name *Aztlán,* an island from which they had started somewhere in the forgotten northwest, was a faint echo as they migrated ever southward, divinely led by their Wizard-God, *Huitzilopochtli*. Generation after generation an elite guard carried their stone God on a litter, a God who commanded them to plant corn and rape and steal and make war and move on to the promised land where they would see an eagle perched on a cactus on an island with a snake clasped in its beak. Sparks shot from his stone eyes if they rebelled, weary of traveling. In return for his guidance he demanded the blood of human sacrifice.

Bereft of a culture of their own and tempered by the need to survive, the *Mexica* had stolen and killed - and observed. Passing through the land of the *Toltecas* they came to the great city of *Tula*, magnificent cultural evidence of the bounty of the God, *Quetzalcoatl*, the Sun-God of the *Toltecas* whose symbol was the plumed serpent, uniting earth and sky. Giant sentinels guarded his temple. This great God had endowed his people with knowledge and skills beyond anything anyone had ever known. And he had once lived among them as a white man who preached against human

---

1 The misnomer *AZTEC* was given to the *Mexicas* by the Spaniards who derived the name from a place the *Mexicas* claimed the original tribe had migrated–AZTLÁN.

sacrifice. The *Toltecas* fell in 1100 A.D., their collapse, to this day, undefined. Two centuries later, the *Mexicas* assimilated the *Toltec* culture, claiming it's history as their own.

Taking note of the impact of *Tolteca* culture upon the region, the *Mexicas* moved on. Soon, from the crest of a mountain, they looked down upon the abandoned ceremonial center of *Teotihuacán*, marked by two monumental pyramids, mounds now covered with vegetation. These people of the Sun had suffered incursions of semi-nomadic tribes and had abandoned their metropolis in 750 A.D., leaving only legends told by the generations.[2] Akin to the *Tolteca, Quetzalcoatl* was also their God. The *Mexicas* took note and pressed on, bearing their own stoic, stone warrior-God in their midst. The promised land still lay ahead, in the place where waters shimmered

1269: It was the year of the New-Fire celebration, the ancient ritual which marked a fifty-two year cycle – and a new beginning.

After a hard days 'walk, Tizoc, a young Mexica warrior, sat on his haunches letting his mind wander as he gazed at the darkening sky. A few scattered clouds, tinged by the disappearing sun, seemed to form lakes of shimmering water. In his imagination he saw a gleaming city of canals and islands forming in the clouds. Were they near their destination? Suddenly a tongue of fire streaked the sky and was swallowed up by the heavenly waters. In a panic Tizoc ran to the sheltering trees.

---

2 To date, archeologists continue to investigate the disappearance of this sumptuous ceremonial site.

In a city of canals, far eastward across the great waters, a young Venetian, charting the sky, felt a surge of excitement as a streak of light flared and disappeared. He came from a family of explorers and dreamed of exploring exotic lands.

In the year 1271, his dream came true. Young Marco Polo set out with his father and uncle to reach the fabled land of China. Traveling by boat, by horse and by foot, scaling mountains, traversing vast deserts, they entered the Empire of Kublai Khan. For twenty-four years they remained as honored guests. Accorded the privileges of Ambassadors, they were permitted to travel and learn all they wished in his Empire. In 1295 they returned to Venice, telling tales of that distant, intriguing land in the Orient and bringing samples of exotic spices and silks.

In Venice, Marco Polo grew restless. Fascinated by the sea, he studied graphs and charts convinced that a shorter route to the Orient could be found by sea. War with Genoa was imminent and he signed on as Captain of a Venetian galley in the powerful Adriatic Fleet. His career was short lived. Marco was captured by the Genoese and thrown in prison.

Another prisoner was thrown in to share Marco´s cramped quarters. He was Rustichello da Pisa, a literate, intelligent multi-lingual young man. And a good listener. For one year he wrote down Marco´s tales of his incredible journeys. When the prisoners were released, Rustichello compiled a book of Marco´s extraordinary adventures.

By 1325 the book had swept Europe, a Europe breaking the chains of Medieval mores.

THE EAGLE AND THE SERPENT

Stealthily, the *Mexicas* had entered the valley of *Anahuac* in 1267 and celebrated the year of the New Fire in 1269. But rest was not yet to be enjoyed. They plodded onward to the fabled place where five lakes were interwoven. Suddenly, a sky of transparent blue was reflected in the waters of lake *Texcoco* as the *Mexicas* stood on the shore and wept with joy. Tall cornfields bore testimony to the presence of powerful city-states which ringed the five interlocking lakes. But the *Mexica's* eyes were on their Priest-Astrologer, *Tenoch*, who pointed to the sign: there, on a marshy island, an eagle was poised upon a cactus, a writhing snake clamped in its beak[3]

They had arrived! Here, they would found their great City of the Gods, *Tenochtitlán*. It would grow. They would plant corn and gather rich harvests. They would rejoice in gold and silver and precious stones and bright feathers. From here they would conquer the four regions of the world. They would build great temples: to *Huitzilopochtli* who had led them from the wilderness, to *Quetzalcoatl*, the Sun-God-Giver-of-Life, to *Tlaloc*, the Rain-God, and to a host of other gods who would govern their daily life. They would sacrifice prisoners and slaves to satisfy the Gods. They would plunder and demand tribute from those they conquered, creating a state whose splendor would know no equal. They would be known as *Aztecs* and they would have dominion over the vast lands of Mexico. It was written.

Wading into the brackish water, the *Mexicas* washed off

---

3 It is not certain it was a serpent; it was a symbol for water and fire.

the dust of their long journey. Then quietly, the insignificant little band slipped into the ancient forest of *Chapultepec* and partook of the sweet, spring water on the hill.

In the year 2-House, 1325, the *Mexicas* put down their first cultural roots. On the island where the eagle had fed, a crude adobe temple was constructed to house *Huitzilopochtli*. They had survived hard years. "Dog people" the tribe was called by the arrogant inhabitants of the neighboring city-states. Ousted from *Chapultepec* they had been driven from desolate place to desolate place. They had been cruelly attacked. But their years as nomads had taught them not to yield to adversity and the dreadful voice of their God had demanded blood for blood! They had proven they were warriors. Finally their enemies had conceded to them a snake-infested, volcanic rock bed near the marshy shallows of lake *Texcoco*, the largest of the five lakes in the valley. The *Mexicas* ate the snakes, rid the area of their menace and began building islands in the shallows of the lake.

On a bright sunlit morning in 1373, Tezomoc, great-grandson of Tizoc the young wanderer, was thatching his roof with marsh grass. His house and those of his clan was on an islet close to shore. It was a good place: fish and water foul and tall reeds abounded. Tezomoc's young wife and the other women were weaving immense mats which later their men would tie to stakes driven into the shallow lake bottom to form a basket-like structure. The mats would wall in a square filled with rocks, wadded vegetation and dirt. Trees would root and corn would soon be planted and harvested on their "*floating islands*". *Already a system of canals linked the cornfields of the clans.*

A high stone temple gleamed in the growing ceremonial center on the main island where twin structures housed their War God and Rain God, dualities which ruled their lives. Only yesterday, Tezomoc and members of other clans had ground mineral colors and finished painting the pyramid-temple in white stucco, trimmed with bright red, yellow and black. The sacred fires had been kindled to welcome the new fifty-two year cycle. Old possessions would be burned. New mats and pottery and grinding stones were ready to be placed in every house. Happily, Tezomoc reflected, his own house, too, would be ready, ready to receive a son, for he would be a son. He worked unceasingly till the Sun God began his night journey.

Without warning the earth shook beneath him. Ashes fell from the sky. Frightened, Tezomoc looked to the heavens. He saw a long tongue of fire race through the sunset. A strong wind made him clutch the roof beams; the water around the islet seemed to boil.[4]

"What have I seen?" Tezomoc shouted.

"What does it mean?" the women cried out.

Across the great waters to the east, Europe had commenced to establish trade with the ancient lands of Genghis Khan. Its wealth and vast size had opened up vistas of a fabulous world hitherto unknown. Now caravans traversed the enormous expanses of Asia fighting the elements as well as marauders to bring back precious objects worth

---

4 Most probably the eruption of the volcano, Popocatépetl.

their weight in gold. Spices, silks, embroideries, carved ivory, lacquer-work and fragile porcelains were sought by the courts of Europe and the new wealthy merchant class. Among the oddities brought back by these traders was a powerful powder: when ignited it burned rapidly, when contained in a capsule it exploded thrusting a projectile into the air which burst into colorful sparks.

> *Before he died, Tezomoc was to see his son wear the robe of High Priest. The long black robe was embroidered with skulls, the hood concealing coarse, matted hair which hung in stiff layers below his shoulders. Glazed eyes pierced a dark, smooth face; a prominent nose gave a look of haughty dignity to his elongated figure. Chosen and schooled to study the calendar and astral signs, all wisdom and knowledge were contained in his head. In his hand an obsidian dagger dripped the precious liquid of life. Obsidian and blood, black and red, darkness and light. The rhythm of night and day must be maintained. Feed the Gods to be fed by them. Sacrifice was a way of life. Slowly the trumpeter raised his right arm and blew into the conch shell, sending a long, mournful note across the canals of Tenochtitlán.*

By the beginning of the fifteenth century Portuguese navigators began to explore the coast of Africa in search of a shorter route to the "Spice Islands". In mid-century a young Genoese was born who learned all he could sailing to the extremes of the known world.

In 1469 the wedding of Isabella of Castille and Ferdinand of Aragon united the two most powerful kingdoms of Spain, forging a single scepter. The might of this sword soon drove the Moors from Spanish soil after 700 years of occupation. It wiped out Islam and unified the peninsula under Christian rule. The Catholic Kings established the Holy Office of the Inquisition as a department of government to strengthen the monarchy and purge the Jewish and Moslem heretics from among their people. "Proclaim Christ or be banished" was the edit. The Holy Office was linked to but not under the jurisdiction of the Pope.

The restless Genoese navigator had read about Marco Polo´s journeys.

He had also studied the theories of geographers and reports of mariners. "By sailing west I shall come to the east" was the conviction that burned in his head. Closely, he had followed the Portuguese. Their new ship, the Caravel, was swift to gain ground against the wind. They had sailed down the coast of Africa almost to the equator (as it would later be known). In 1488, Portuguese navigators had rounded that tip of land to sail on to India, Indonesia and China. – the coveted Orient. Portugal considered itself the owner of the trade route with the Orient. . The sand was running through the hour glass. Christopher Columbus knew there was a shorter route. He had a mystic belief in his destiny. He must set sail! He must find a patron to finance an expedition.

In 1477 Columbus had journeyed to Lisbon, the liveliest city in Europe. The King of Portugal had listened to his scheme ... and turned him down. "It is costly and impractical" the King´s experts advised. The phrase echoed through empty years. In 1482 Columbus presented his plan to Isabella and Ferdinand but war with the Moors absorbed the Spanish Kings.

1469: Aztec astronomers studied a newly discovered constellation of stars that pointed unequivocally east from Anahuac. What lay beyond the great waters to the east, they pondered? Did danger lurk there?

Drums beat, skiffs clogged the canals, people wailed in the great square of Tenochtitlán. In 1468 Moctezuma the first had succumbed. During his thirty-year reign, this astute statesman-warrior had expanded the Aztec Empire east of the snow-covered volcanoes to the Gulf of Mexico, and by water route to the far off Maya Kingdom of Yucatán. Later he led his army into the valley of Oaxaca, some 800 miles southeast, and subjugated the *Mixteca* kingdoms of that rich region. Moctezuma´s cunning equaled that of Machiavelli´s: on the pretext of trade, he would assess the strength and wealth of the targeted city, establish ties, then launch a surprise attack, conquer and demand tribute. Sacking villages, stealing women, beating and humiliating the vanquished, the new rulers were feared and hated. The victorious armies returned to Tenochtitlán triumphant, leading long lines of bound and yoked captives whose fate was to become slaves or sacrificial victims. Once a city was conquered, garrisons were established to carry out Moctezuma´s orders.

Great wealth, in the form of tribute, began to pour into Tenochtitlán: gold, silver, coveted jade, obsidian, precious stones, lumber, lime for building, vast amounts of textiles, feather work, delectable seafood brought up from the coasts by runners, pearls, pots of honey, avocados and tropical fruit, tobacco for the Lords´ pipes, shrubs, flowers, flowering trees for the gardens of the nobles, animals for their menageries, exotic birds for the national aviary, quilted armor and other regalia of war. On and on. A much-prized tribute was the cocoa bean from which chocolate is made, a product widely used as barter.

In little more than one hundred years the lowly *Mexica* had risen to Lords of the land.

Under Moctezuma the First there was an explosion of work. With no beasts of burden, the human back and dugout canoes were the means of transportation. Work on the great temple was continuous. Each succeeding ruler had covered the old walls with a new outer wall, increasing its size. But floods and years of famine had often halted the work.

The Gods had doted one man with extraordinary intelligence and ability: *Nezahaulcoyotl*, King of Texcoco from Toltec lineage, kinsman and ally of Moctezuma. A skilled engineer, he devised a system for controlling flood waters: a dike was constructed that ran nearly ten miles; the three broad causeways that connected the island-city to the mainland were constructed on pilings and converted to levees which divided the saline water from the fresh waters of lake *Xochimilco*. Plans were made for aqueducts to bring sweet water from the springs of Chapultepec. King, engineer, diplomat and poet, *Nezahaulcoyotl* sponsored a university for philosophers and poets within his palace. A follower of the teachings of the enlightened God, *Quetzalcoatl*, he came to abhor mass sacrifice and built a shrine to an omnipotent spirit he called "The Lord of the Everywhere". No images could represent this deity since his home could not be fixed.

The body of Moctezuma the First was cremated with his slaves and buried. A young, vigorous King, *Axayacatl*, was selected to ascend to the throne of the exalted "First Speaker". In an attempt to spread the Empire northwest, *Axayacatl* was defeated by the powerful *Tarascos*[5] in a devastating battle. He was succeeded by a brother who marched straight north into poor, useless territory and died in disgrace soon after. Under his successor the Empire expanded but the Aztec armies were now engaged as much in putting down rebellions as conquering new city-states.

In 1485 the priest-astrologers made note of a brilliant star in the constellation that pointed east.

Across the waters, in Extremadura, Spain, an infant emerged from his mother´s womb with a lusty cry. They named him Hernán Cortés.

---

5 The correct name for this tribe is "*Purepecha*". "*Tarascan*" was the name mistakenly given by the Spaniards.

CHAPTER II

CORTES AND MOCTEZUMA

Moctezuma the Second, grandson of Moctezuma the First, was born under mystical signs.[6] When the Chief Magician had rolled out the book of fate, it was shown that his good auguries would place the infant boy in a position of leadership, but not without extreme trials. He would be a warrior of high rank. He would exercise justice. His wealth would fill vast treasure houses.

The young boy was selected to be schooled in the *Calmecac*, a privileged monastery of the highest learning where gifted young boys were taught calendar-science, picture-writing, history, war tactics and proper speech in *Náhuatl*, the correct language for speaking to visiting chieftains and the Gods.

While Moctezuma was being groomed for high office, the great city of *Tenochtitlán* was undergoing fervid

---

6 Moctezuma The Second, Xocoyotzin, Ninth Huey, Tlatoani or Emperor.

construction to rise to its peak of grandeur: an improved system of levees, completed dikes and aqueducts, movable bridges that opened or closed the causeways, depending whether for friend or foe. Painters applied fresh coats of white stucco, trimmed in bright terra cotta, blues, black and yellow, to temples, palaces, the great library, markets, schools and low flat-roofed houses. The awesome *Teocalli*, a pyramid-shaped temple which housed the Gods of War and Rain, rose 160 feet, dominating the ceremonial center of *Tenochtitlán* and dominating the lives of its subjects and all people under their dominion. Garrisons of warriors were stationed throughout the provinces, creating a chain of communication from the great waters of the east to the great waters of the west, and through the jungles to the far south. The rhythm of sacrifice was beating faster and faster on the temple drums. The treasure houses were filled with riches. But the priests were uneasy: as they searched the heavens and studied their calendars and magic books they saw portents of disaster. Along the three causeways streams of prisoners entered the island city. At the feast of the dedication of the enlarged temple hundreds of prisoners were sacrificed to the insatiable Gods.

In despair, on a bitter January morning in 1492, Columbus had set out with his young son en route from Spain to the court of France. As the sun set, the full moon shone brightly over a nearby monastery. Cold and exhausted, Columbus and the boy made their way to the Franciscan Friary and stopped there to rest. They were welcomed by Friar Juan Perez. The good man listened with interest and compassion to the disillusioned Genoese. The Friar had been confessor to Queen Isabella and arranged an audience for his visitor with the Catholic Queen. Columbus reached Granada in time to witness the surrender of the last stronghold of the Moors in Spain. Flushed with victory, Isabella received the zealous navigator. Wealth and trade filled her vision. Making an impetuous decision, it is said she sold her jewels to finance his voyage.

Financed by Isabella and with a letter to the Grand Khan in his possession, Columbus and eighty-eight adventurous souls prepared to sail into the unknown. Their guides were the stars and a compass. The sails of their three small ships were set toward the setting sun. The year was 1492. In the year 1502, Columbus made his last voyage to the Americas.

In 1502 Moctezuma the Second, ninth ruler of the Aztecs, ascended to the throne of First Speaker. The setting sun had long been the preoccupation of Moctezuma and generations of his ancestors. It was upon the sun that life depended. He rose in the morning , made his great journey through the sky, then disappeared in the unknown regions of the night. There he had to struggle with his twin brother for survival so that he could rise again, triumphant, the next morning. One was born with a debt - to keep the Sun God alive. They were locked in mutual dependence: feed the Gods to be fed by them.

As was foretold at his birth, Moctezuma was a good ruler. He was grave and sober of character, just in his dealings, feared and respected by the people. With valor, he led new campaigns toward the Pacific coast, consolidating east and west. But intrigue and rebellion dogged his path. There was discontent and a bad omen in the wind. On his fourth and last voyage, in 1502, Columbus had made contact with the *Maya*. The story of a strange apparition in the waters off Yucatan, "Like a moving mountain in the sea", carried through jungles and steep rises across the mountains to Moctezuma´s ears.

"Wars of Flowers" with the neighboring states, waged for the sole purpose of capturing prisoners for sacrifice, were turning into real battles. His fury mounting, Moctezuma attacked his neighbor, Tlaxcala, and was defeated. The war continued.

A few years later, from the roof of his palace, Moctezuma saw a comet so bright it lit up the sky and "seemed to bleed fire, like a wound in the sky." What did this omen foreshadow?[7] He summoned his astrologers and soothsayers. They had seen no comet. Outraged, he had them thrown into cages.

Other portents of disaster followed: snow fell on Tenochtitlán. On a windless day, gigantic waves boiled up in the lake and broke over the levees. A two-headed child was born. In 1515 a new phase of war with Tlaxcala began. But defeat followed defeat. Moctezuma´s captains were stripped of their rank and honor. Even worse news was that there was division in the ranks of his ally, the great city-state of Texcoco whose Chieftain and Lords were kinsmen.

As a boy, Herrnán Cortés had been intrigued by mariners' stories of Columbus' voyages and the new islands that lay on the other side of the world.. Caught up in the fervor to go to the Indies, at the age of 19, young Cortés had left family and home in Spain to begin a new life on

7 Trying to explain the unexplainable events.

the island of Española. He resided there seven years as a Colonial Minister and landowner. In 1511, he joined Diego Velasquez on an expedition that conquered Cuba and claimed it for Spain. Soon recognized as the jewel of the New World, Cuba became flooded with Spanish adventurers. Expeditions across the narrow stretch of water to the west had proven there was a long and solid mainland ahead. The Captain of one expedition, Juan de Grijalva, returned from Yucatán in 1518 with tales of a fabled Empire and gold artifacts to prove its existence. Hernán Cortés listened carefully and determined to explore the mainland. For eight years he had waited in Cuba for this opportunity. Now, his hour had come. Thirty-four years old, of good stature, robust, and an astute politician, Cortés was a man of note. He was a seasoned horseman and swordsman, a fervent Christian and Latin scholar who had attended the University of Salamanca. He could read the Book of Prayers written in Latin.[8] The newly probed mainland became an obsession with Cortés. He had the unwavering belief that he was fated to conquer the unexplored Empire. Like Columbus, a sense of mission drove him. In this belief lay his greatest strength.

With cunning and diplomacy, Cortés obtained written authorization from Governor Velasquez to captain a large exploratory expedition. Sensing that the Governor was about to rescind the broad-termed authorization, Cortés secretly sailed from Cuba under cover of night. Eleven ships comprised the fleet; the force was made up of 608 men: sailors, soldiers, musketeers, crossbowmen, a few black

---

8 The first known book to have reached Mexico was a prayer book discovered in the Yucatan Peninsula.

men, a priest, the well-born and rough adventurers. In addition, 16 horses, 5 dogs and 10 cannon were put aboard.

With a favorable wind, the fleet soon crossed the 160 miles to the shores of Yucatán, home of the descendents of the great *Maya* civilization.

Resolute purpose filled Cortés while fear gripped *Moctezuma.* Cortés was prepared to use muskets and cannon at the slightest provocation if the people were hostile.

The fates had a better plan. They bestowed upon Cortés three unexpected gifts: two interpreters and a mystical date to land on the shores of Mexico, 1519, the Aztec year One-Reed

Hearing of "moving towers in the sea", a Spanish sailor, shipwrecked in an early expedition, made contact with the fleet and was picked up by Cortés at the tip of Yucatán. Gerónimo de Aguilar had been a captive of the *Maya* for eight years and was fluent in their language.

After an encounter along the southern coast, in which the natives, armed with clubs and arrows, quickly capitulated to the thunder of the cannon and deadly spears of the man-beasts which ran swifter than deer, their chieftain gave the white visitors twenty women slaves. Among them was a high-born young woman who had been sold into slavery to the *Maya* by her Aztec mother and spoke both *Maya* and *Náhuatl,* the Aztec tongue. She was called *Malinche* and in her heart she harbored resentment for the Aztecs.

Mysterious forces wove their spell: with his two interpreters Cortés was able to communicate with all whom he encountered.

Cautiously exploring the coast, Cortés led his fleet into a protected channel in a harbor which they named Veracruz, place of the True Cross. There he proclaimed the land for King Charles V, planted the Spanish flag and with his men sank to his knees in gratitude and prayer.

Moctezuma was consumed with anxiety. Thirty dishes were set before him at every meal and his bitter cocoa served in a cup of fine gold. But he had lost his appetite. His Lords kept their heads bowed in the presence of his semi-divine person, unable to speak until spoken to. On his fevered brow, Moctezuma felt the hand of doom. Reports had come to him of the landing of white men in the great waters to the east. Mysteriously, tongues of fire had flared up in the temple of a Goddess blackening the blood -crusted walls and destroying the sanctuary. For several nights the panic-stricken people heard a woman's ghostly voice wailing across the canals, "My children we must flee from this city. Alas my children, where can I take you? Where can I hide you that you may not be lost forever?" [9]

"Quetzalcóatl is angry," Moctezuma's most trusted adviser stated, looking at his sovereign directly in the eyes. "You have made him a lesser God."

Moctezuma bowed his head. Secretly he retreated to a cave where he beseeched an oracle: "What am I to do? Why has this terrible disaster befallen me?"

The oracle spoke thus: "I am Quetzalcóatl, the plumed serpent, the greatest of all the Gods. I am the

---

9 The legend of "La llorona" (the crying lady) is still told in Mexico and some claim they hear her wailing in the night.

giver-of-life, closest to the sun, like the eagle, and closest to the evil caverns of darkness beneath the earth, like the serpent. I commanded you to build a fitting temple to the Plumed Serpent as did your forebears the Tolteca and the Mixteca and the Maya and the Olmeca. Did I not promise to guide the sun safely through darkness? Did I not live among you as a man, with spun rays of sun for a beard, guiding and advising and teaching you all the days of my life? Was I not opposed to sacrifice? You have exceeded this practice! When I was tricked and cast myself away from your shores in the great waters of the east, did I not promise to return in the year One-Reed?"

Moctezuma prostrated himself and wept bitterly. The year One-Reed came only once a century, and this was the year. "Are these your people, oh great and mighty God? Have you returned?"

The oracle did not answer.

Moctezuma made his decision: he ordered the finest raiment be sent to the god-intruders, the finest woven robes, necklaces of gold, jade masks, beautiful feathered capes and head-dresses. Their leader was to be presented with the accoutrement of *Quetzalcóatl* himself. Ambassadors were dispatched with instructions to welcome the gods with all the respect they deserved. "I am but the custodian of their domain," Moctezuma said humbly. Secretly, he hoped these gifts would halt their march to *Tenochtitlán*.

A magnetic force seemed to propel Cortés westward toward the mountains. And the Fates bestowed upon him yet another gift: allies. Thousands of discontented Aztec vassals joined him on his march from the coast to the fabled City of the Gods.

Cortés was a leader of rare genius. Endowed not only with physical courage and military prowess, he also had a talent for diplomacy and a sense of vision. That he was filling a messianic Aztec prophecy he would learn through his Indian interpreter, *Malinche*. His own role as Captain of this Spanish force he saw in a messianic light. Conversion was his duty and baptism the means. The idols of these people were demons! Their temples reeked with the fumes of hell! In an early encounter, with reason and tact, through his interpreters, Cortés tried to convince the leaders of a coastal city to give up their cherished ugly, squat idols. He showed them an image of the Virgin Mary holding her child, the only Son of the only God. They alone should be worshipped. A piece of wood! The chiefs scoffed and continued their human sacrifice. Incensed, Cortés ordered their sacred idols smashed. When they saw their Gods tumble in pieces down the temple stairs, chiefs and priests wept bitterly. Cortés´ goddess was stronger. Lowering their heads, they accepted baptism and their new position as vassals of the King of Spain.

The first to be baptized was *Malinche*. Intelligent, noble and of graceful mien, she had made her choice between the obsidian dagger and the iron sword. She was baptized with the Spanish name of "Marina" and was married with Catholic rites to one of Cortés´ captains. In less than a year she was speaking Spanish, now the sole, indispensable translator for the returned God, Cortés. Later, she was to bear the Conqueror a son.

As they explored the coastal region, idols toppled,

people wept. Defying fear of the white gods, Eagle and Jaguar knights led their troops into battle. But iron swords, horses, fierce dogs, iron suits of armor, iron cannons, iron muskets, ... and an iron will overcame their numbers. Reasoning that these gods would overcome Moctezuma, many more joined their ranks.

Now, with several thousand under his command, Cortés prepared to march over the snow-whitened pass from which an 18,000 foot peak rose. Spurred by the promise of gold, most of his men were willing to risk their lives. But there were dissenters among the crews. Cortés made a momentous decision: he sent one ship back to Cuba with letters for Governor Velasquez and King Charles V, along with two natives and the magnificent gifts sent to him by Moctezuma. Then, it is said, he ordered the other ten ships burned.[10] The die was cast. There was no turning back.

Spaniards fell in battle, tied up their wounds, and slept in battle dress with their sword at their side as they marched inland from tropical shores to heights where cold, rain and hail added to their discomfort. Apprehensive, ever watchful, they approached the realm of Moctezuma. A fateful moment was their entry into the region of *Tlaxcala,* Moctezuma´s undefeated and mortal enemy. Outnumbered by a vast army, Cortés´ men assembled in battle formation. Making the sign of the cross, they waited for the attack. Horses, unknown to the natives of the Americas, superior morale, superior weapons and superior battle tactics gave the Spaniards the strength to break the massive Indian ranks and rout them. When the *Tlaxcalans* saw that their ritualistic defenses were ineffective, they lost courage and,

---

10 He didn´t burn his ships, he merely dismantled them.

although their Chief warned against it, they soon joined the ranks of the allies. As allies of these strangers they could destroy Moctezuma*!*

Cortés´ army increased. On the long marches, the Spaniards baptized thousands of natives. Anyone who refused to renounce his evil gods for the Christian cross was baptized by force and branded. On they marched - "a multitude raising a great dust, some encased in iron, swords shimmering, resounding from afar" wrote the priest, Sahagún. As they approached the sacred city of *Cholula*, center of the cult to *Quetzalcóatl*, the Spaniards were warned of a treacherous ambush planned by Moctezuma. So it is told. Whether true or not, when a throng gathered in the courtyard of the revered God, the Spaniards and their allies massacred thousands.

News of *Tlaxcala´s* alliance with the strangers and the massacre at *Cholula* struck dread into the hearts of the *Mexicas,* "as if the earth trembled beneath them, as if the world were spinning before their eyes." Whether human or divine, the invaders had demonstrated their power. Desperately, Moctezuma tried to stop their march with lavish gifts of gold which his Ambassadors reported "they fingered and seized like monkeys." He sent members of his council, sorcerers, his trusted nephew. To no avail. In Cortés´ mind "exploration" had translated to "conquest." He had received word of the backing of Governor Velasquez and King Charles V.

On a cold November morning, nine months since his departure from Veracruz, Cortés led his army through the pass between the two great volcanoes that guarded the valley of *Anahuac.* Spanish soldiers raised their heads to look at the overhanging snow covered peaks above them, then peered down through the shifting clouds into deep and fearful precipices below. As they descended from the summit and emerged from the forest, awesome was the sight they beheld: Through the mist, the gleaming white city of *Tenochtitlán* lay below them, its reflection shimmering in the waters of a large lake. Other cities dotted the sunlit valley, but Spanish eyes were fixed on the Capital of the fabled Aztec Empire, more beautiful than any city any soldier had ever seen. Spellbound, they descended into the valley.

Against the advice of his Council of Four, Moctezuma decided to welcome the invaders. Within a few days they arrived. Canoes jammed the canals, crowds jammed the square and the rooftops as the strangers approached along the grand causeway. Curiosity and terror struck the people dumb. In silence they watched the exotic procession: leading the parade, astride a white horse, rode their leader, his face hidden by a strange shining hat; behind him rode a standard bearer, followed by lancers, crossbowmen, cannon, dogs straining at leashes, helmeted soldiers in suits of armor astride restless horses, an animal that to native eyes seemed to blend with the man. An endless stream of allies followed, crowding into the spotless, sacred ceremonial center of the great *Tenochtitlán.*

Borne on his royal litter, Moctezuma awaited his guests at the end of the causeway. Behind him towered the main temple with its twin shrines. "The temple was part of a vast complex formed of seventy-eight buildings and capable of holding 10,000 people at a time", Bernal Díaz, a soldier, was later to write. Moctezuma descended from his litter. Supported by four richly dressed lords, the great Emperor slowly advanced "beneath a marvelously rich canopy of green feathers, worked with gold and silver, pearls and green stones which hung from a kind of border which was wonderful to see. He was richly dressed and wore shoes, like sandals, with soles of gold and covered with precious stones... Many lords walked before the great Moctezuma, sweeping the ground where he would pass, and putting down mats so that he would not have to walk on the ground. All kept their heads down, with great reverence," Díaz described the scene.

When Cortés saw the great Moctezuma approaching, he quickly dismounted.. The sun reflected from his helmet like a mirror as he removed it and bowed with reverence and respect. An orator recited the long, sonorous *Náhuatl* welcome speech. "Then Cortés gave the great ruler a necklace of glass beads, strung on a golden cord. He placed it around Moctezuma´s neck and was going to embrace him when the princes accompanying the great Chief caught Cortés by the arm so that he could not do so, for they thought it an indignity," Díaz continues.

Moctezuma then spoke: "Our Lord, you have wearied yourself, but now you have reached your own land. You have arrived at your city, *Tenochtitlán*....No, I am not dreaming, nor seeing visions. I have in truth seen you and have now set eyes upon your face.... Come to our land. Come and repose; take possession of your royal abodes. Come to your land, O lords," Díaz quotes.

The final act in a long and controversial drama was about to be enacted.

As though to announce to all neighboring states that turmoil engulfed Moctezuma´s Empire, in 1519 great spirals of smoke rose from the crater of *Popocatépetl* and ash was belched from his fiery center. Astounded by the spectacle, Cortés reported the event in his letter to the King of Spain.

Whether feigned or sincere, Moctezuma played the magnanimous host. Cortés and his men were quartered in the palace of Moctezuma´s father, a labyrinth of halls and rooms and courtyards and gardens and aviaries. Hundreds of slaves were assigned to their every need. They were given free rein of the city. It was evident that Cortés was a man of flesh and bone. Impressed with the advanced techniques used by the Aztecs, in a letter to Charles V, Cortés remarked: "The observations and intelligence of these natives is far superior to the Caribbeans (among whom he had lived for sixteen years). Many natives of this land could easily be assimilated into Spanish society."

Moctezuma soon learned that it was gifts of gold that lighted the eyes of Cortés´ men. To further appease this craving, Moctezuma lavished gold gifts upon them. For the Aztec, delicate gold jewelry and artifacts were linked to the Gods.[11] By wearing gold jewelry or having a gold image of one of the gods in your home, one was linked to God-given energy. The Spanish soldiers melted their gold "trinkets" down to bullion. With freedom to roam the premises, they soon discovered the secret, formidable treasure house in the palace. The rough adventurers were staggered by the sight of such riches.

Guided by a mystic sense of guilt, Moctezuma had

---

[11] Gold was considered the gods´ excrement and had a ceremonial, not an economic value.

changed directions: a relationship of respect and near-affection developed between the two demi-gods. In vain Moctezuma´s Council advised against fraternizing. In their talks, Marina, ever at his side, Cortés tried to dissuade Moctezuma from continuing the practice of sacrifice. But the great Chief´s religious zeal was as fanatic as Cortés´. He explained that there was a code of ethics in sacrifice. In no instance did it imply a feeling of hate or cruelty. Once a captive was made prisoner or a man was chosen for sacrifice, he considered himself chosen by the Sun and thus specially honored. In death he was united with the great Sun God, becoming, in effect, his son, a status held high by the victim himself. Many prisoners when offered freedom, preferred sacrifice. Moctezuma took pains to explain that on no account was it a sin to sacrifice, on the contrary it would be a sin not to; man´s sojourn on earth was a fleeting one and his manifest destiny was to keep the Sun in the sky. Such a fatalistic philosophy and high regard for death were beyond Cortés´ ability to understand. Aztec cruelty and brutality had driven allies to his camp.

Excursions around the city entertained the Spaniards interest for awhile. Visits to the great market of *Tlaltelolco* revealed a seeming endless assortment of goods and food: corn, beans, squash, cactus leaves (*nopales*), tomatoes, avocados, chiles of many varieties, maguey worms, grasshoppers, meat from fat little dogs, a variety of birds, armadillos, ducks, rabbits, mounds of tortillas and tamales, dried fish caught in rivers and coconuts brought from the coast. Cacao beans (the source of chocolate) were sold only to rulers as was woven cotton cloth. Peasants could only wear clothes woven from maguey fiber. Visits to the zoos and botanical garden where medicinal herbs and plants were classified, also captured the Spaniards admiration. Special expeditions to the gold mines awakened lust and visions of great wealth. But nerves grew taut: they were guests, not victors. They felt their safety was in jeopardy in the confines of the city. Wooden draw bridges on the causeways cut off their access to the mainland. No longer regarded with fear, they saw hostility in eyes that stared. Hostility turned to fury when Cortés´ tough, redheaded Captain Pedro Alvarado, fired on a singing, dancing assembly of temple celebrants and massacred 3000 people. Cortés was away. He returned to find a howling horde trying to ram the door of his men´s compound

In a daring move, Cortés and his captains seized Moctezuma and held him prisoner in their palace. With utmost tact and patience Cortés tried to convince Moctezuma to give up his idols and be baptized a Christian. Moctezuma was resolute in his refusal. In a fit of anger, Cortés and forty of his men climbed up the blood- stained stairs to the temple of *Huitzilopochtli* where, with a mighty blow, Cortés struck the fierce God between the eyes with a crowbar.

All hopes of appeasement, all thoughts of a bloodless conquest shattered into pieces. A holy war began.

Rocks were hurled down upon the Spaniards, javelins and arrows met them each time they ventured out. Shrieks and insults echoed. The Spaniards rolled out their cannon, slashed with their swords, but the rain of rocks was more deadly. To the victorious beat of drums and trumpeting of conch shells, Spanish captives were marched up the temple stairs and sacrificed. Escaping to the roof of the palace,

Moctezuma tried to subdue his subjects only to be met by a barrage of stones, hurled with might and fury. He was stoned to death.

The battles raged. Now desperate, Cortés ordered his men to escape to the mainland under cover of night. But they would not abandon their booty - gold. Burdened with gold bars the Spaniards were trapped on the causeway. Bodies clogged the bridges, gold fell into the lake. Two hundred Spanish soldiers lost their lives. On that "night of sorrow", Cortés wept as he watched those captured being bound and lined up for the short trek to the temples.

THE SETTING SUN

Powerful *Tlaxcala* gave haven to the beaten Spaniards. Soon *Texcoco* and *Tacuba* , which had formed Moctezuma´s triple alliance, submitted to Spanish lure. Reinforcements arrived from Cuba. In another nine months Cortés was prepared for the siege of *Tenochtitlán*.

Brigantines were built, sails mounted and cannon fixed to the decks. Strategy was mapped to cut off the enemy´s supply of fresh water and food, to blockade their canals, to fill in the gaps in the causeways for access to the city ... to burn the houses, to target their captains and generals. But no military strategist could foresee the ferocity and valor with which the Aztecs defended their sacred city.

Eighty days the siege lasted. Cannons blasted from the lake. Canals turned red with blood, fires raged, darkening the sky with black smoke. A great plague broke out; smallpox, brought from Europe, spared neither warrior nor new Emperor.

Moctezuma´s successor died and young *Cuauhtémoc* was named to replace him. The battle raged until there was not a weed to eat, not a dart or rock left to throw. Violence within. And violence without. Corpses piled up in the streets, the houses, the canals. Thirty thousand *Aztecs* are said to have died. Twenty thousand of Cortés´ allies were killed.

"I have read about the destruction of Jerusalem, but I do not think the mortality was worse than here in Mexico," are the words of Bernal Díaz, who was there.

The whirlwind that had swept over ancient Mexico for two years died out with a painful shriek when *Tenochtitlán* fell. The last Emperor, young *Cuauhtémoc*, is said to have asked Cortés for his dagger: "We are vanquished. Kill me," he begged. Instead Cortés held him prisoner and tortured him to reveal the hiding place of Moctezuma´s legendary treasure. It has never been found. Eventually *Cuauhtémoc* was hanged.[12]

Wounded in body and spirit, a fallen Eagle Knight sat midst the ruins of the great *Tenochtitlán* and remembered the teachings of the Gods: It was not here truth was to be found, it could only be found beyond the tangible, the visible. A poem of *Nezahualcóyotl* was the last thought to cross his mind:

> "We have come only to sleep
> We have come only to dream
> Our body is a flower

[12] A regal statue of Cuauhtemoc now stands on the Paseo de la Reforma, a main avenue in Mexico City.

That blooms and withers
For life is an ephemeral gift
And this world is not permanent

Today, in "The Plaza of the Three Cultures" in Mexico City, site of the last battles fought between Spaniards and Aztecs, a plaque reads:

"ON 13 AUGUST, 1521, TLALTELOLCO, HEROICALLY DEFENDED BY CUAUHTE-MOC, FELL INTO THE POWER OF HERNAN CORTÉS. IT WAS NEITHER A TRIUMPH NOR A DEFEAT, BUT THE PAINFUL BIRTH OF THE MESTIZO PEOPLE THAT IS THE MEXICO OF TODAY."

CHAPTER III

NEW SPAIN

1521

In Europe, another Empire was being vanquished by the force of a single man: Martin Luther was banished by the Catholic Church. The Holy Roman Empire, whose popes had exercised absolute power over life in Western Europe for approximately three centuries, was beginning to weaken. Luther´s famous ninety- five indulgences had unleashed social, political and cultural changes on a static society. It was a time of Reformation.

1521: King Henry VIII of England began proceedings to place the Church under the authority of his Crown, thus breaking with the Pope. Protestant England was soon born.

1521: In Spain, an uprising by commoners demanding constitutional rights was defeated by the nobles, increasing the power of Charles V, the Hapsburg King who had brought the Netherlands, Austria and Germany under Spanish rule. Added to its Italian possessions, Spain´s might was unrivaled in Europe.

1521: In the far Pacific, Magellan reached the Philippine Islands and claimed them for Spain.

1521: Michelangelo finished his monumental work in the Medici Chapel in Florence.

An age of enlightenment, of re-birth, gave creative impetus to the arts, to new inventions, to new laws, to a new, bold consciousness of secular life and individual rights. And to new discoveries. The horizon was always in front.

THE FRENZY OF CONQUEST:

After 1500, like a tide, Europe assaulted the globe in a frenzy of expeditions to establish and dominate trade routes. It was a one-way process; only the Turks and slaves entered Europe. Although ancient cultures were superior in many ways, the Europeans felt superior as possessors of the true religion and masters of the seas. They were contemptuous of the values and achievements of the people whose cultures they altered or destroyed. Once the Portuguese had rounded the tip of Africa and Columbus had discovered America, to control the flow of exotic goods from east-west became the obsession of the Crown heads of Europe. Fire-power was their major asset. Although the Chinese had known about gun powder for centuries, it was advances in European metallurgy that produced formidable artillery. Turkish galleys, relying on slave-oarsmen to propel them, and poorly armed Chinese war junks were no match for sleek merchant ships with guns mounted broadside. Psychologically, the Europeans were ready to explore, open to a future of change and adventure, whereas old cultures fought to remain insulated even from neighbors with whom they had traded for centuries. For more than a century the Portuguese led the way for European trade with North Africa and Asia, their firepower sweeping all before them as they built up a chain of fortress-bases in the Orient. As early as 1513, the Portuguese had reached the Spice Islands (the Moluccas) and pressed on. They seized islands claimed by Spanish explorers until only the Philippine chain was left to the Spanish Crown.

Once Columbus had established a route to the Americas, a rush to form and finance expeditions from the Spanish-held Caribbean islands consumed the minds of investors, navigators, soldier-adventurers and the Spanish Crown. Columbus´ belief that he had reached the "Indies", islands described by Marco Polo as forming the eastern extremity of Asia, was soon discarded, but the native American would forever be known by the misnomer, "Indian". While Portuguese navigators reached out farther and farther in the Orient, Spaniards were driven to find a route through or around the recently discovered mainland. Spanish ships set sail up and down the coastlines. When the riches of the Aztec Empire were revealed. gold became the song of the siren.

The first half of the XVI century was an era of momentous discoveries and conquests: Early in the century, Amerigo Vespucci had sailed down the continent of South America, giving a name to the New World. By 1511, Spain had established a crucial base in Cuba. In 1513 Vasco de

Balboa crossed the Isthmus of Panama and discovered the Pacific Ocean. That same year Ponce de León discovered Florida. While Cortés conquered *Tenochtitlán*, Fernando de Magallanes (Magellan) sailed down the eastern coast of South America and navigated through narrow straits near the tip of the continent into the immensity of the Pacific Ocean to discover the Philippine islands, named for King Phillip of Spain. From Mexico, Cortés marched south and soon conquered the old Mayan Kingdoms of Guatemala and Honduras, establishing "Captaincies" in these new provinces. Sailing down the Atlantic and southern Atlantic oceans, the Rio de la Plata river was discovered and later a settlement called Buenos Aires established. On foot the Spaniards crossed the mighty Andes into Chile. From Panama, they moved south, claiming the territories of Colombia and Ecuador, then up to the dizzying heights of Bolivia and Paraguay. In the northern continent, the Spanish conquerors moved north and west from Florida to the Mississippi river. Expeditions led by Cabeza de Vaca, Hernando de Soto, Vasquez de Coronado and others consolidated territories north of Mexico from Florida to California. The Spanish reached Virginia on the Atlantic coast where they found neither great mineral deposits nor encountered extensions of native farmland. To subdue nomadic tribes was not in their immediate interest. The Pacific coast promised greater benefits. They explored as far north as Vancouver, Canada, giving names to a series of small islands. Early in the century the English had begun exploring Labrador and the Hudson river, obsessed with finding a northwest passage. It was not long before a French expedition, led by Jacques Cartier, was exploring Canada.

In 1528 there was jubilation in Spain when news reached the King that Francisco Pizarro, departing southwest from Panama, had discovered an Empire similar in riches to the Aztec. Centered in the Andean mountains that rose from the narrow stretch of Peru, the *Inca*[13] Empire had controlled the mountain chain and its fabulous riches for centuries. Pizarro finally vanquished the *Inca* in 1533 in a treacherous act, accepting gold for clemency, then executing their last King.

By mid-century the psychosis of conquest was over. The existence of a new, lengthy continent, divided from Europe and Asia by vast stretches of ocean on each side, was recorded in crude maps. With the exception of Brazil in the southern hemisphere, claimed early in the century by the Portuguese, and the northernmost territories in the northern hemisphere, claimed by France and England, Spain was the owner of the new world called simply "America". Its natives had been killed, died of disease, or reduced to virtual slavery.[14] In some sparsely populated areas, such as Costa Rica and Argentina, the native population was almost totally annihilated. And in Chile, where the natives remained in the high Andes, conquerors and Indians remained separate.

The conquests were a trail of blood let by savage brutality. Intolerance and racism led to subjugation and repression of the native American.[15] The tough, assertive Spanish

---

13 Erroneously named Incas. It was the Quechua and Aymara empires. Inca was the name assigned to a main leader or a title.

14 Indian slavery was prohibited by the New Laws in the testament of Queen Isabela of Spain

15 Not everything was destroyed and much of the Indian way of life remained.

soldier of fortune neither intended nor tried to understand native cultures. Violence begat violence. But the fiber of those men who sailed in small ships, whose small expeditionary forces endured extraordinary hardships, knowing not where they were going or what they would find - who crossed the Sierras and the Andes burdened with heavy arms and armor, cannot but be noted. Many died, some deaths as cruel as those they inflicted. America, it is said, was conquered with the sword and the cross.

Once America had been discovered, the march of man could not be contained. **The earth is flat. No, it is round.** The jolt to man´s image of himself and the ground upon which he stood was forever changed. The globe emerged and the knowledge that all people, everywhere, live upon the same planet.

After the night of conquest, earth and sky were in dense darkness, so dense that lightning could only penetrate as a flicker, leaving not a whisper of sound in its wake. It was a darkness which promised no dawn. When the sun weakly overcame night, it cast a gray veil over ruined temples and a cold wind began to seep up alleys and lash the waters of the canals of Tenochtitlán.

After the last battle, after breathing the stench of death and viewing its ruins, numbness shrouded the mind and heart of conquered and conquerors alike.

Victory was a vacuous silence. Then, like an arrow that finds its mark, a recurrent thought pierced Cortés´ brain: How would these vassals of Spain be governed? It was calculated that the valley of Anahuac, heartland of the Aztecs, had a population of about a million and a half. And there were other tribes, other city-states to subdue.

Conquest was one thing; governing the conquered another. How should this land be administered? .

The Aztecs wept. "They have killed our Gods, they have killed our dance, they have killed our song. Where will we go? Who will guide us?"

Celestial fires died out in the milky river where stars clustered and the Moon Goddess fed. An era of enlightenment swept Europe but New Spain was born in twilight, the rekindled twilight of feudalism

With his uncanny ability to gain advantage of every situation, Cortés secured from the Spanish Crown the title of Governor General of New Spain. To build a capital city was his first priority: he ordered colorful geometric temples to be torn down and their idols destroyed. The rubble was used to fill in the shallows of the lake. A Spanish city was soon under construction. It was called simply "Mexico." The plan defined an immense central square, flanked by arcades; it included a Cathedral, a Legislative Palace, a market, a convent-school, a hospital and Cortés' own palace on the site of Moctezuma's. This center was to be inhabited exclusively by Spaniards, the four outlying wards to be governed by Royal Indians related by blood to the lineage of Moctezuma. Such an explosion of work induced Friar Motolinía to write; "there are more laborers at work here than can be counted, more than raised the Temple of Jerusalem." Native craftsmen were quick to learn to use the new iron tools. By 1524, geometric forms had been replaced with flat, Romanesque structures. In front of where the great temple-pyramid had stood, native sculptors were finishing the intricate facade of a baroque Christian church. The same brown hands that had carved serpents and idols were now carving fat angels and lean saints. Slowly the old civilization was buried under the new. But history crawled among the buried rocks guarding the old culture.

Conversion of the Indian had been accepted by Cortés as a solemn duty. He understood that the conquered Indians lived in a spiritual vacuum. Religion had ruled their lives. Where were the choruses of boys and girls dancing and bearing flowers at feasts to honor the Gods? "The very stones cried out so great was the pain," wrote Friar Durán. Eyes that had once been bright with expectation were now dim, sad, lowered. Wearing a self-imposed mask, they did what they were told and went where they were told. Through silent submission they sought to enclose their pride, keeping it untarnished, concealing their humiliation. Cortés dispatched a passionate plea to King Charles asking him to send missionaries to instruct the natives and "save their souls." In Europe, the Pope was being thwarted by Luther's followers. The New World offered Catholic evangelists the opportunity to resume their sacred apostolic crusade.

The first missionaries to arrive were three Flemish Friars, followed by twelve Franciscans who walked barefoot over the mountains from Veracruz. These humble men of God were greeted with amazement and respect by throngs of Indians who were accustomed to the arrogant and cruel demeanor of the conquerors. Even Cortés knelt to kiss an emaciated hand. By 1536, other missionaries had arrived: seven Augustinians and twelve Dominicans. Thanks to these mendicant, educated Friars who set about learning the native *nahuatl* language much of Aztec history was preserved. The great library of *Tenochtitlán* was destroyed at the request of the first Bishop in his fervor to curb the pagan culture. "We sacked the city but found nothing of value so we burned the great house where all the chronicles of their ancient things were stored," Cortés reported to Charles V.

In the month of December, at dawn in the year 1531, Juan Diego, a devout and humble Indian convert, set out from Mexico to hear Mass. The morning star shone brightly, brighter than he had ever seen it as he approached the hill of Tepeyac where lay the ruins of the temple to Tonantzin, ancient mother of the Gods.

"He heard sweet singing, like a chorus of birds", a scribe quoted him. Then a woman´s voice called him by name, luring him up the hill toward the ruins. At the summit stood a lady, "her garments shining like the sun, the rocks on which she stood emitting rays of light, converting dull cacti into leaves of lustrous green," the scribe faithfully wrote of the miraculous appearance. Overwhelmed, Juan Diego asked himself, "Am I dreaming?" Then she spoke:

"Juan, Juan Dieguito, I am the Virgin Mary, the mother of the only Son of God, He who is the only Giver of Life, the Creator from whom all things come, the Lord of heaven and earth. I desire that a temple be built for me here. Here I will offer my love and my mercy to all those who dwell in this land and invoke my name. I will listen to all their lamentations that they may find healing for their pains and sorrow. Go

to the Bishop of Mexico and tell him all that you have seen and heard. Go."

Stunned, Juan Diego ran to do her bidding. "I have seen the Mother of God!" he told Bishop Zumárraga, but the Bishop scoffed and asked for proof Crestfallen, Juan returned to his village.

The following week, on December 12th, he again had to cross the hill of Tepeyac en route to the convent of Santiago where his uncle lay dying. Again, the Virgin appeared to him.

"Your uncle is totally healed," she told him. "Now go and tell the Bishop to build my church."

Miraculously, white roses were strewn in his path. He gathered them up in his mantle and took them to the Bishop. When Juan opened his mantle in the Bishop´s palace, the roses spilled out, and there, on the rustic fiber cloth, just as he had described her, was an image of the Virgin.

"The brown Virgin" of Guadalupe soon became the patron saint of Mexico. Today, her image on Juan Diego´s mantle is enshrined in a new, modern church. Millions of worshippers make a pilgrimage to her shrine every year on December 12, designated by the Catholic Church as her saint´s day. In the courtyard, plumed dancers circle, layers of shells tied round their ankles rattling in a never-ending rhythm marked by the beat of drums. Moors and Christians battle each other in dance, the new and old religions blending. (Note: The Archbishop´s Palace where Juan Diego revealed the Virgin´s image on his mantle is today a museum. Recently, Pope John Paul 11 canonized Juan Diego, accepting as true his miraculous encounter with the Virgin. The mystery of the Virgin of Guadalupe´s imprint on his well-preserved mantle continues to baffle scientists and non-believers alike.)

Whether or not an Indian had a soul had been questioned by the Church due to their practice of human sacrifice, cannibalism, homosexual customs, concubinage and other scandalous practices (It is alleged that Moctezuma had more than a hundred concubines). In 1537 Pope Paul III issued a Bull recognizing Indians as rational beings and therefore subject to baptism in faith. In the second half of the XVI century thousands of Indians were baptized, often under threat, torture and a minimum of instruction, leaving doubt as to whether the convert was praying to St. Michael or *Huitzilopochtli*. The terms "Christian" and "person" became synonymous, bonding Church and State as they were bound before the conquerors arrived.

The first hundred years were marked by ardent missionary zeal. A new pantheon, cloaked in European Christianity, superseded the old. The death rites of the Aztecs had ingrained a fatalistic attitude in the native. The old liturgy celebrated death, the new liturgy celebrated life. To the Aztec, life and death were aspects of the same reality; the dead were, in essence, "undead", having simply passed from one plane to another. What differences had not been resolved in this world would be faced and resolved in the next. To be in harmony with the Gods was the purpose of life. Now, there was only one God, a Divinity made Man who came to redeem man from his sins and eternal death. Christ promised a burden-free existence in the life hereafter.

The Cross was the way, evil was punished in the fires of Hell and Heaven was the reward of the good. Saints replaced idols. Instead of a legion of gods, there was only one, a God who had sacrificed himself for them. Aztecs found intercession through the priests. They needed consolation and this is the triumph of Catholic Mexico.

The missionary, Pedro de Gante, saw in music a form to embrace the new doctrine. Born in Flanders in 1480, first cousin of Charles V, theologian, humanist, musician, he established the first school of music in the Americas (1523) on the edge of Lake Texcoco.where a burst of activity was transforming *Tenochitlán* into New Spain. Indian voices joined Spanish voices to form a choir, and Indian drums learned to mark new rhythms to glorify the new God.

As Governor of New Spain, Cortés was caught between two conflicting interests: the Crown of Castile, eager to impose order and justice, and the demands of his own men. More adventurers followed, out to make a quick profit.

The Aztec agrarian system divided the land among clans; a man worked for the community. Now all the land belonged to Spain. Under pressure to establish a mode of governing, Cortés installed the *encomienda* system, a land "trust" which did not confer title. As practiced in feudal times in Spain, a grant of *encomienda* entrusted a large given area to an *encomendero,* "trustee", who was charged with the Christian welfare of those who lived on his estate as well as its defense. This permitted the *encomendero* to bear arms. Those for whose welfare he was responsible paid him tribute in material goods and labor and he, in turn, paid revenue to the state. Unless controlled, the system was open to rampant abuses. Huge tracts of land were given to Cortés´ soldiers. Thus thousands of Indians were put under control of a few rough, uneducated Spaniards. Abuses were heaped upon abuses and excessive brutality was often exercised: an angry *encomendero* would cut off the hand of an Indian who failed to work as demanded, or rebelled or was slow to produce. Frequently he branded his Indian vassals to keep them from escaping.

Whether to assuage his conscience or help keep the Indians subdued, Cortés accorded encomiendas to former Aztec Lords. He married Moctezuma´s favorite daughters to his Spanish officers, never soldiers. The Kings of Tlaxcala and Texcoco were given authority over their own cities. Thus were Cortés´ allies rewarded.

The native served as field hand, beast of burden, household servant, concubine, a virtual slave. Cortés had little control over his *encomenderos* some of whom were abusive to the extreme. Early on, the King had sent salaried officials to help Cortés administer his new possessions. Soon alarming reports of rebellions, more abuse of the natives and rampant corruption reached the King. He realized that New Spain was in a state of near anarchy. (Note: It was not until 1570 that the encomienda system was completely eradicated.)

King Charles V was a young man, aware of human frailties, but he was a strong, devout Catholic. He believed that his divine right as King obliged him to rule with justice. New Spain was an extension of Mother Spain.. It must be ruled by an extension of himself - a Viceroy. Viceroys were ruling the immense Austro-Hungarian Empire Charles V, as heir, had brought to the Spanish throne. His new

Viceroy must be a well-educated man of integrity, intelligence, high morals, and ability to rule and develop the vast territories of the new world. He appointed a panel of judges to examine his chosen candidate.

Every one of the sixty-two Viceroys who governed New Spain had to be approved by the King´s panel of judges. Those who proved excellence in governing were moved to Peru to become the Viceroy of the King´s second most important territory. A few were recalled for misconduct or mismanagement.

The first Viceroy, Antonio de Mendoza, arrived in New Spain in 1535. His subjects were a mere 1000 Spaniards and about three million Indians. Of all its American possessions, Mexico was the most heavily populated. A few years after the arrival of de Mendoza, disillusioned, pushed to one side, Cortés returned to Spain, was assigned to Charles V´s failed military attempt to capture Algiers and died, without fanfare, in 1547.

Cortés entered history in Spain´s moment of ascension to power. When he landed on the shores of ancient Mexico, *Tenochtitlán* had reached its zenith and discontent was creating fissures in Moctezuma´s Empire. Like Columbus before him, Cortés was driven by a sense of mission. And like Columbus, he accomplished his mission. He was a key player in Europe´s intrusion, and ultimate destruction of the world of the native American. With contempt, some refer to Cortés as the progenitor of the mestizo race, and Malinche, his concubine, a traitor. However he is judged, astute leadership and personal valor cannot be denied.

Much has been written about Cortés and Moctezuma,

two powerful men with very distinct visions of the world. Their transit through history marks the transition of Mexico into a mestizo nation, Latin by definition. In an early will, Cortés requested that he be buried in the land he conquered. After numerous exhumations in Spain, his bones finally came to rest in Mexico City, in the Hospital of Jesus which he founded. There is no statue to Cortés in Mexico. For many, his name is anathema. For defenders of the indigenous people, Cortés is a beast as depicted by Diego Rivera´s murals in the Palace in Mexico City. The Conquest happened. It is a fact. Once America was discovered, the Aztec Empire was destined to fall. I often wonder what Mexico would be like if the British had been the conquerors.

CHAPTER IV

THE KING´S BOUNTY:

From the beginning, gold had been the lure of the conquerors but it was Mexican silver that kept the coffers of the kings of Spain filled for 300 years.

Silver and gold were extracted by the Aztecs primarily from visible veins which ran down or alongside a mountain. Following a vein downward through a mine shaft was the method used by Europeans. With the advent of pumps and drills, shafts gave more rewards. Several shafts could be connected deep in the bowels of the earth creating great cavernous underground chambers.

The second half of the XVI Century saw a rash of mines being discovered and developed. Silver mania infected both King and his subjects. The driving force was Indian labor. Most mine owners were *encomenderos* who had the right to use the Indians on their lands. As mine shafts were dug deeper into the mountain, the harrowing work of the miner was brutal. The work was organized by squads headed by *barreteros* (foremen). Under them, peons opened tunnels, extracted the ore with a crowbar (*barra*) and filled *tenates* (hide bags) with the ore. The load was lifted onto the back of a *tenatero* supported by a strap around his forehead. Some loads were as heavy as 180 pounds. Once secured on his back, the ,*tenatero* started his long, circular climb up through the shaft, climbing hundreds of narrow steps carved into the sides of the mine shafts, up, up to the opening at ground level. They worked in shifts of eight to ten hours. A misstep and man and cargo plunged back into the depth of the mine often taking with him his companions a few rungs below. "I have witnessed scenes that surpass Dante´s Inferno", one Friar wrote. To most early Indian miners, death was a welcome friend.

As mines opened up farther and farther north - Querétaro, Guanajuato, Zacatecas, Durango - the *Chichimeca* Indians continually harassed the Spaniards and their mule trains loaded with silver for Mexico City. The invaders were invading their territory! Never subdued by the Aztecs, these tough, nomadic Indians attacked the Spanish settlements without mercy. From 1550-1590. wars with the *Chichimeca* were never ending. Captured *Chichimecas* were sold to the miners as slaves. To counteract their growing number, friendly Indians were brought in to fight with the Spanish soldiers and relocate in the invaded territory. This immigration of central tribes who spoke different languages reinforced Spanish as a common language. The Spanish rewarded the immigrants with better working conditions: pay, a bonus and the privilege of taking out a bag of *pepena*, (fragments of ore) which they could sell or "reduce" for its silver content. By the end of the century the *Chichimecas* had been almost absorbed into new populations.

Deep ruts made by heavy wagon trains freighting through canyons and mountains were the first primitive roads. In mid XVI century, to supply the mining communities, a road was built from the Capital as far north as the great mining town of Zacatecas. Called *El Camino Real*, time worn cobblestone stretches can still be found in the beautiful colonial cities of the Bajío, the central plateau. Later, El Camino Real was extended into the province of *Nuevo León* with the foundation of the city of Monterrey. It would continue to California linking branches along the way.

Immediately after the discovery of America, Pope Alexander XVI had issued a Bull bequeathing all lands discovered and to be discovered to the Catholic Kings of Spain whose duty it would be to convert the heathen indians. Just three years after the conquest the missionary work in New Spain began. Missions were of necessity self-sufficient and vitally important throughout the colonial period.

The vast northern territories of New Spain would always pose a problem: desserts, spiny shrubs, heat, bitter cold and hostile Indians hampered the Spanish thrust north. Only the very adventuresome would leave the temperate climate of the central plateau where water, food, flowers and greenery abounded. It was the missionaries who settled the north, men with a zeal to evangelize and civilize. Monasteries and missions soon sprang up all along the Camino Real. The missions were established to subdue and gather native populations into towns so they could then be converted to Christianity and learn to live in a society which would ensure their survival.

The Jesuits were the first to carry the cross to far regions. With a sprig of wheat tucked in their prayer book, early on they were establishing missions on their trek northwest. A prime driver of the Jesuit movement was Father Kino. In 1687 he started colonizing the vast territories of Sonora, Sinaloa, Arizona and parts of California. He discovered that Baja California was not an island as indicated in early maps but a peninsula.

In the annals of history it is doubtful that the vanquished were so vociferously defended by such an array of saintly scholars. Foremost among them was Friar Bartolomé de las Casas, a Dominican and himself a former wealthy *encomendero*. In his fanatical defense of the Indian he became a power at the court of Charles V. He questioned the rights of Spaniards to be "given" Indians. He even questioned the right of the Crown: "For sixty years they have been robbed and tyrannized. What obligations have these innocent, unhappy people to fill the needs of the Crown of Spain?" The Council of Indies, established in Seville in 1524 to administer all affairs of New Spain, soon enacted protective legislation and sent special commissioners to carry out the new laws.

Education was an early concern: the sons of noble Indians and Chieftains became students of Latin, logic, mathematics, philosophy and theology. Convent schools were established to teach young Indian women to read. In 1551 the first universities were established in Mexico and Peru. The first printing press in the Americas had arrived in Mexico in 1537.

Spanish ships arrived on schedule in Veracruz, transporting missionaries, nuns, architects, philosophers, fine Renaissance tapestries and furniture, animals, merchants, all manner of supplies - and Inquisitors. New Spain began to look like "Mother Spain." Unlike the English colonies, New Spain was not a colony, it was an extension of Spain itself. Conquest and colonization were not the same. New Spain was administered as a viceroyalty. The Viceroy´s charge and obligation was to protect the King´s property so that it could produce. The Viceroy had all the authority of the Crown; his was the voice of the King. Although the term "Colonial Mexico" is widely used it does not mean "colonial" in the context of the self-ruling English colonies which were granted a "Charter" by the English Crown to establish their settlements. In Mexico, the word "colonial" refers to its 300-year period under Spanish rule.

During the XVI century, slaves, captured by the Portuguese, had begun to arrive from Africa to do the hard field work. By mid XVII century the physiognomy of the Mexican was changing. Among the racial mixtures, there were sixteen official castes: at the top of the list were the *criollos* (creoles), children of two Spanish parents born in Mexico; there followed *mestizos*, children of Spanish-Indian blood, and last, *mulatos*, a combination with African blood. Spain, itself, had endured invasions by Phoenicians, Romans, Celts, Visigoths, and seven hundred years of Moorish occupation, hence Spaniards were accustomed to a multi-racial society. The classification of "castes" denoted neither religious nor legal restrictions; it was used simply to identify bloodlines in New Spain. A person's caste was determined by the grade of crossbreeding between European, Indian and African blood. Later, his "caste" came to determine a person's social rank.[16] The need for slaves was brief in Mexico and blacks as an ethnic group disappeared through intermarriage.

After slavery and the *encomienda* system were abolished, to keep Indians on their large ranches (*haciendas*) or mines, the "peon", as he was known, was kept in eternal debt.. Generations worked on the same *hacienda,* born with the burden of their father's debt. The *hacienda* store was the sole source of available goods: lard, wheat, sugar, cloth, a bucket, a hammer. The owner was the provider and the peon's future wage his guarantee of payment. Much like the cotton plantations in the neighboring north, it was a never-ending debt system which guaranteed a labor force. In 1576, a typhus epidemic decimated the Indian laborers on the immense agricultural and cattle *haciendas* in the northern provinces and forced immigration from central tribes who spoke a different tongue, again reinforcing Spanish as a common language. Thus was a nation being slowly built.

At the top of the social structure were the *peninsulares*, Spaniards born in Spain. They alone were entitled to hold positions of high authority. In 300 years no more than 300,000 Spanish settlers arrived in New Spain, few of them women. *mestizos* were below *criollos* but above pure Indians. They became servants, shopkeepers, soldiers, artisans and

---

16 The paintings of the different "castas" were made during the 18th century, Age of Enlightenment, where plants, animals and humans were studied and classified.

small landholders. *Mestizos* were subject to the Inquisition as well as civil courts.

The face of the land, too, was changing. Herds of cattle, goats and sheep now grazed among the maguey plants The maguey, agave, was God´s gift to the native Mexican. It had been their source of parchment, sewing needles, thread for cloth and twine. At maturity, it provided a sweet, milky liquid , *aguamiel*, rich in protein, which babies drank to make them strong. When fermented, the sap produced *pulque*, an intoxicating drink, God's elixir for the over-worked peon.. Corrals now confined teams of horses. The 16 horses brought to Mexico by the conquerors were the first horses in the Americas. Wild horses, their descendents, migrated north to be tamed and bred by northern Indian tribes. Mules, donkeys, oxen, pigs and chickens now shared a Mexican farmer´s patch of earth where before only wild pigs, small dogs raised as meat, an occasional deer and wild turkeys had trespassed. The receding lakes created marshland where crops of rice were planted and wheat germinated rapidly in warm soil. In addition to the corn tortilla, a hard-crusted bread roll was added to the diet. Onions and garlic became staples in the Mexican kitchen where lemons, apples, peaches, lettuce, carrots, parsley and spices from the orient led to rich provincial dishes. Although corn, beans and chiles remain the basic staples, sugar and lard, in particular, transformed Mexican cooking. Flowing from the new world to the old, corn, tomatoes, potatoes, squash, avocados, vanilla, pineapples and cocoa beans were among the array of new foods added to the European diet. Today, the cuisine of Mexico is as varied and exotic as the country itself.

Intent upon converting the indigenous population, by mid XVII century the great missionary drive had created growing settlements in the provinces.

Schools and hospitals were run by the religious orders and the Spanish language superceded native tongues. After the first hundred years, the interest of the Church shifted from conversion to education – and ownership of land.

Once the cross was firmly planted in America, Spain looked from her Pacific shores toward the west to find a shorter passage through the southern seas to the coveted riches of the east. The remote group of islands in the far Pacific Ocean, discovered by Magellan and known as "The Philippines", became Spain´s Asian bastion. They named the capital Manila, a magnificent port, and walled it from intruders.

After the Conquest, when the Capital of New Spain had risen on the ruins of *Tenochtitlán*, Cortés himself set out for the Pacific, traveling almost due west. Native guides led his small band of explorers over the rugged western Sierra Madre, winding down from pine forests and rocky valleys to deep, hot canyons and luxuriant tropical vegetation. Suddenly... there it was, the Pacific ocean, blue waters stretching to an infinite horizon. Cortés looked upon a bay that surpassed all expectations, an immense horseshoe protected by hills. The harbor could contain the whole Spanish fleet! The Spaniards´ mutation of the native name of this incredulous bay was Acapulco. Spurred by his insatiable drive to explore and conquer, Cortés sent for shipbuilders and set out in the first ship to explore the ocean. Shipwrecked, attempting to round the treacherous foot of a peninsula (to be called Baja California he gave name to that narrow sea and established the port of San Sebastian – today La Paz.

Skilled native hands, with native wood and Spanish shipbuilders, built the first merchants ships that traversed the vast Pacific from Acapulco to the Philippines. For centuries, the Philippine Islands had been a cultural crossroads for trade among Chinese, Malay, Hindu and Japanese merchants. By 1571, Manila was a walled, bustling port ruled by a Spanish Governor, her streets crowded with Spanish soldiers, priests, officials and merchants who traded in a dozen languages. Warehouses were filled with exotic goods. Philippine shipyards began building larger, sturdier and superior-rigged ships out of teak and other more resistant woods. These queenly galleons, known as "Naos de la China", enhanced the Spanish Crown with envied riches. Mexico became a land bridge between the ports of Cadiz, in Spain, and Manila, virtual gateway to Asia. The fabled Spanish galleons set the course for trade between three continents, Asia, America and Europe, exceeding the dreams of Marco Polo and Columbus of opening a trade route to the Orient.

The galleons´ voyages spanned 9000 miles in each direction and often took a year to make the round trip. Until the *tornavuelta*, rapid east-to-west trade winds and currents, was found to guide navigators over the tortuous eastbound route, the proud "Nao de la China" would arrive in Acapulco with a toothless, emaciated remnant of its crew.[17]

---

17 The "tornavuelta" was discovered in 1571 and Acapulco, San Blas and other   ports developed strong ties with the Orient

The first landfall usually sighted was in Alaska, then down the coast to Cape Mendocino in northern California where missionaries took baskets of oranges and lemons to the scurvy-ridden crews. Along the length of California, missionaries planted orange groves to serve the galleon trade when it was discovered that citrus was an antidote to the dread scurvy. A century or so later, lemons were rationed to British sailors by decree, origin of the nickname, "limey".

From the mines of Zacatecas, Pachuca and Guanajuato, a stream of Mexican silver flowed across the Pacific. Silver became highly prized in Asia as a new material for artifacts. The Mexican silver dollar, marked with a Chinese "chop", became the economic power of Asian trade. Mexican silver paid for the prized eastbound cargo overloaded with forged ironwork, chests of perfumed sandal-wood, lacquer desks, jade objects, fine porcelain, silk and cotton textiles, ivory carvings, a range of tantalizing spices, gold filigree jewelry. Small boats jammed the harbor of Manila as merchants from Borneo, Cambodia, Malaya, Siam, India and China made their way to the Philippine Islands to export their goods. Many ivory crucifixes and saints that adorned the halls of the Inquisition were carved by the heathen in China.

The eastern cargo was auctioned in Acapulco, the bulk destined for other Spanish galleons waiting in the port of Veracruz. The westward cargo from Spain arrived in Veracruz. It included much-sought and needed European goods embarked from Seville and Cadiz: manufactured leather goods, textiles, glassware, fine furniture and the latest fashions. Raw material shipped from New Spain came back as finished products: cured leather returned as shoes and cotton returned as cloth. Westbound passengers were merchants, settlers and zealous priests whose new mission was to convert the heathen in the Philippines. Trading halfway round the world, through middlemen and officials, the "China trade" bred smuggling and corruption.

Corsairs roamed the waters; the Spanish galleon was the world´s greatest prize. If not prey to pirates, typhoons and unchartered reefs sank many of these "Queens of the Sea". In the 250 years of the China trade (roughly 1570-1820), forty ships failed to arrive, their treasure stolen or buried in briny depths along the route.

The "Nao de la China" sailed from Acapulco in January and with good luck returned in October. With the ship securely anchored, the grand auction in Acapulco began: The Crown´s administrator unloaded the cargo, charged the King´s "fifth" (20 %) and other local taxes, then permitted bidders from Peru and Europe to vie with Mexican traders for the coveted treasures. South American goods departed from Acapulco down the Pacific coast by ship, goods slated for Spain and purchases destined for Mexico City were loaded on pack mules for a trip through scorching canyons, pine forests, up to craggy cliffs and down into valleys as the "China Road" cut through the southern Sierra Madre to the port of Veracruz on the Gulf of Mexico. Other mule trains, delivered silver bullion to be minted in Spain. Towns like San Miguel El Grande (today San Miguel de Allende) along the route became stopovers where animals, muleteers and the military guards were fed, housed and rested. From Veracruz, Spanish ships sailed with their prize cargo for Cadiz, on the Mediterranean, once again prey to pirates who hid out along the Spanish Main. Francis Drake, a notorious British pirate, was knighted with the title of "Sir" by Queen Elizabeth for his daring raids and siege of Spanish treasure ships. Robbery of the Spaniards was considered by the English as a holy war against the Pope.

In 1587 Sir Francis Drake destroyed much of the Spanish fleet at Cadiz and in 1588, in an attempted attack on England, Phillip II of Spain sent his mighty Armada against his Protestant enemy, Queen Elizabeth. In a devastating naval battle, with the weather in favor of England, the great Spanish Armada was sunk.

In 1580 Portugal had been united to Spain and was soon to lose her Orient trade. The Dutch United East India Company established commercial supremacy in the Orient bringing about the collapse of Portuguese control. All source of profit shifted to Dutch hands. Burned and ravaged hulks floated aimlessly from the Indian Ocean to the China Seas. Soon, French and Dutch fleets began appearing in the Caribbean. Using captured islands as their base, they raided as far south as Panama where Inca gold was embarked. Deals were struck by buccaneer captains to share the booty and kings secretly encouraged them to break the Spanish monopoly on western trade. Silver coins from the mines of Mexico became the currency of the flourishing commerce. The Spanish "piece of eight", or peso, was known as a "dollar" by the English-speaking people, a term derived from a 16th-Century Germanic silver coin called "thaler".

By the time Independence was won (1821) Mexico was providing two thirds of Spain´s revenue. The "Naos de la

China" left an indelible mark on a world opening its eyes to new horizons of goods and cultures.

> *1620: Juan Perez Apatzin returned from the corn-field to his thatched hut and dropped down on a straw mat. His wife was on her knees on the earthen floor fanning a brasero on which a pot of beans was cooking; beside her a stack of warm tortillas was wrapped in a cotton cloth. She rose and poured him a jug of* pulque *then another. Soon he would be drunk. The milky, fermented liquid from the maguey plant, venerated by his forebears and only permitted to be imbibed during festive celebrations, was his only escape from a life of never-ending toil and tedium. Sitting on a homemade wooden chair, his oldest son watched the smoke rise and escape through the roof of the kitchen lean-to.*
>
> *Suddenly a streak of lightening illumined the hut followed by the crash of thunder.*
>
> *"The Gods are grumbling," Juan remarked in* nahuatl *. A votive candle flickered under a picture of the Virgin of Guadalupe. "Blow it out, woman!" he ordered. From a sisal knapsack he pulled out the stone figure of the old rain God, Tlaloc, and gently rubbed it. "Tlaloc is watering the corn."*
>
> *"I tremble to think what would happen if Father Rodrigo knew we are harboring stone idols," his son said in Spanish.*

One hundred years had passed since Cortés had laid siege to Tenochtitlán.

CHAPTER V

The thunder rolled down from the north where heavy clouds shrouded the Atlantic seaboard. far up the coastline. At the northeastern extension of the continent, a storm miraculously veered off course from a sheltered bay to allow a band of pilgrims to land in territory claimed by England. Seeking religious freedom, 101 men, women and children disembarked from the "Mayflower" on a cold December morning in 1620 with a charter from the English crown In 1621, one hundred years after the Spanish conquest of Mexico, Plymouth Colony was founded. The "Mayflower Compact" assured the equality of all men before the law and the voluntary subordination of all individuals to the society. Followers of John Calvin, the reformer who had broken with Rome nearly a century before, individual rights and self-government were basic tenets of their belief. Purists and separatists to the core, these "Puritans" were to have a lasting effect; New England became the citadel of puritan North America. Dutch and French Huguenots, fleeing religious persecution from Catholic France, soon crossed the ocean and established colonies on the same northern seaboard. Trade-minded Swedes obtained permission from England to settle in the new world. Though different in interests and character, the colonists were Europeans of a similar culture, united in their zeal to defend and extend their freedom of religion and self-government. Gradually, they accepted English as a common language. The administrative head of a colony was an appointed Governor; under him a Council, or Assembly, was elected by the townspeople. Boundaries and use of land were determined at town meetings and the Council was empowered to collect the Crown's taxes.

Like Mexico, New England became fertile ground for products with trade value in Europe. Sugar had arrived in Mediterranean-Europe from Africa early in the millennium but even in the late 16th century was considered a luxury. The propitious climate in the Caribbean had turned the islands into fields of sugar-cane, planted and harvested by fragile natives. The Caribbean islands soon became plantation societies dominated by a few white Spaniards. Sugar was also an important product of New Spain. Cortés, himself, had been engaged in sugar plantations in the Caribbean before moving to Cuba. His two sugar mills in Mexico were the first on the continent. Hard labor and disease soon decimated the frail native populations of the Caribbean. The toll on the population was devastating: two thirds of the native population died from overwork and transplanted diseases in the first hundred years. The worse scourge was smallpox.

As the native populations diminished and the European demand for sugar increased, Portuguese traders began bringing over a sturdier race, African slaves. The lucrative slave trade was sold to exclusive French and Dutch companies which began supplying the Spanish settlements of Haiti, Dominica, Cuba, Jamaica, Puerto Rico and New Spain. The Spanish received the slave ships in their West Indian islands and sold them to the English colonists. Chained in squalid, crowded conditions, thousands of black captives died before they reached the auction blocks. Thousands more died of starvation, cruelty and disease. Unscrupulous slave traffickers amassed fortunes. In the English colonies extensive tobacco and rice plantations were taking root along the southern seaboard. Later, large cotton plantations thrived in the south, again increasing the slave traffic. Between 1680 and 1786 it is estimated that more than two million African slaves were sold to the American colonies. Bookshelves are filled with the injustices committed in this inhuman traffic in humans – people seized without warning, divested of every possibility of defending themselves or communicating with their families, beaten, starved, treated and traded like "goods", a chapter in human history written in hell....

To break the Spanish yoke off their coast, the English fleet seized one island after another. English bases were established on the islands of Jamaica, the Bahamas, Barbados and Trinidad, and on the mainland, Belice and what became British Guiana. The French and Dutch were close on their heels. The Caribbean was the busiest route of travel in the western hemisphere, rife for espionage and battle, its small islands affording perfect hide-outs for pirates.

Who controlled the Caribbean controlled the riches of the world. Until 1898 Cuba, the jewel of the Caribbean, and Puerto Rico remained well-defended Spanish strongholds.

The XVII Century had made its entry inauspiciously in New Spain. The seasons came and went on the high plateau of Anahuac. Moctezuma´s manifest destiny, to keep the Sun God alive and thus ensure the continued existence of the universe, was superceded by Spain´s manifest destiny to save souls, settle the new land and extract her riches. The sun continued to rise in the morning and set in the evening while the names of the old Gods became but a faint echo in the jungles. Spanish was the new tongue and Catholicism the new religion. These two factors, language and religion, were making unification possible.

In Mexico, the Archbishop ruled almost side by side with the Viceroy. Conflicts between Church and State flared into uprisings in a continuous tug for power. In a famous rift, a culprit took refuge in a convent and a civil authority tried to arrest him. The civil authority was accused of violating the immunity of the Church. A battle for supreme authority between the Archbishop and Viceroy caused riots in Mexico and eventual recall of both to Spain and dismissal from their posts.

Early in their reign, Isabella and Ferdinand instituted the Inquisition to wipe out heresy. Arab mosques and Jewish temples had dotted the landscape of Spain for seven hundred years. Now, one country, one religion under Catholic rulers was the credo. Be converted or be exiled was the law. The Inquisition was a link between the Civil Government and the Church but under the jurisdiction of the Crown not the Pope. It had absolute autonomy and immunity. Civil courts were never allowed to question the procedures and decisions of the courts of the Inquisition. The Inquisition had the sole right to investigate, discover and punish heresy. A person could be suddenly arrested without recourse, their properties and possessions confiscated, thrown in jail and tortured without ever knowing who his accuser was. Spread through France, Germany Italy and England since medieval times, the worst practices of the Inquisition were adopted in Spain. It was a fearsome arm of terror. In New Spain, an anonymous accusation denouncing a person as a Jew, a witch, a Protestant or simply as the owner of a Bible or a forbidden book, even having missed Mass one Sunday without a proven excuse, could lead to arrest. Only the Indians were not subject to the Inquisition as Rome had not yet determined whether they had the ability to reason and whether they had a soul. The Holy Office of the Inquisition was instituted in New Spain in 1571. In the annals of New Spain, 1596 stands out as the year in which the most offenders were arrested.

The clanging sound of the Palace clock jarred Pablo awake at 5:00 a.m. He rushed to awaken his wife and children. Hurriedly they dressed and picked up their blankets, crucifix and oil lamps, eager to get a good place in the crowd. It had started. Juan and his family hurried to the street. Headed by the Viceroy, the long procession came into sight. Surrounding him, his august Ministers brandished their golden canes. The Archbishop and Inquisitors followed holding high their fearful standard, the green cross. A solemn line of the members of the Tribunal paraded ahead of 108 prisoners; nine, it was said, would be burned at the stake. "They're coming, they're coming" Pablo's younger son pronounced in a muffled shout as the family pressed forward. Pablo shuddered and jostled his way through the crowd.

Minor offenders were hanged first then tied to the stake and burned. Cardinal offenders were burned alive. In 250 years, only a small number were burned alive and about 300 hanged. In Spanish America, the Inquisition protected the dogma of the Church, more a watchdog over behavior and morals than a force of terror

The Church never found ways to adapt to progressive ideas. The Inquisition was not abolished until 1820.[18]

With such immense territories to control, the administration of New Spain was a rigid, centralized line of command. The Viceroy, appointed by the King, had jurisdiction over all administrative matters pertaining to New Spain. Under him and appointed by him, the *Audiencia*, was his Judiciary Council. Each province was administered by a Governor, also appointed by the Viceroy. A local council (*Cabildo*), composed of judges (*Alcaldes*) and councilmen (*Corregidores*) was presided over by the Governor. Judges visited the territories and a special solicitor, selected by the local council, represented the people. Merchant Guilds (*Consulados*), regulated all commerce. In the Capital, a *Consul*, appointed by the Viceroy, was in charge of all goods that entered and left the country. Spain imposed a tribute

18 The House of the Inquisition in Mexico City, with its torture chambers is today a museum.

on her subjects, Indians included, and goods entering or leaving a given province paid a customs´ tax at the border.

The Viceroy reported to the Council of Indies, across the ocean in Seville, a council created to administer all holdings and advise and orient the King in all matters pertaining to his possessions in America. In its three hundred years of Spanish rule, there were excellent Viceroys, men of vision who helped the country to prosper and effected legislation to correct its ills. There were also corrupt Viceroys, men bent on personal gain. The King appointed men he considered of integrity and wisdom as his Viceroys but since it took three to four months for messages to be sent and received between Spain and Mexico the way was open to corruption, contraband and countless irregularities. Tax collectors, royal officials, collected "two fingers" more.

By decree in 1680, the Council of Indies jurisdiction over books was reinforced. It became the judge of which books could be freely sent to New Spain: romances, histories, essays, books of art, of philosophy, even astronomy were prohibited from free transfer. Although the first printing press in America had arrived in Mexico in 1535, the Council of Indies had control over what was printed. Only books of Christian virtue should be read by educated colonial subjects of the Crown. The literate Indian seldom read anything beyond the catechism. Homer, Virgil, Dante, Copernicus, Góngora, Cervantes could be found only in the libraries of a few privileged families, the erudite court and religious institutions.

José, grandson of Juan Perez Apatzin, had married well. His wife, a mestiza had produced a light com-

plexioned daughter who attended the parochial school. María Isabel, was a pious girl whose intelligence had won the attention of the parish Priest; he, himself, had taught her to read.

"She wants to enter the convent," her mother announced. "As you can see, books attract her more than men."

José and his wife were devout Catholics but they understood little of the ritual Mass preached in a language not even of the conquerors: Latin, a language their daughter was learning

"I will light a candle to St. Francis," José replied, "and pray that she be accepted". To have a son or daughter in the Church was a matter of prestige. Many young women of the upper classes were entering the convent.

"Make sure that she takes Father Alfaro our fattest chicken. And the cheese I made yesterday, his favorite," his wife reminded him

Inside the walls of a convent, one of New Spain's most intelligent women penned her famous poetry. In 1689 the poems of Mexico's first lady of letters were published as part of a magna three-volume work which would confer on her the title of "Muse of America." Sor Juana Inez de la Cruz was a nun whose personal library reached four thousand books. Born in 1651, Juana could read by the age of three. A beautiful young girl, and a creole, she had been educated at the court of the Viceroy. Her intelligence had been put to the test by the erudite court in a verbal dissertation which had proven her astounding fund of knowledge and ability to reason. Long theological and philosophical quotes in Latin amazed her audience. The Viceroy compared the encounter to "a regal Galleon being battered by a fleet of skiffs." Science and religion were not separate, she expounded, if a humanistic goal inspired them. Her consuming desire was to study and write. It was considered enough for a woman to read only what was useful for the salvation of her soul and health of her body; beyond that women did not need instruction. Socially, there were three classes in Juana´s day: The Ecclesiastical, the Court, and "the people." It was frowned upon for a woman to express an opinion, and certainly not to ever question; "if they wish to ask a question let it be to their husbands within the walls of their home." Where but in the convent, protected by a nun´s habit, could she satisfy her compulsion to study? Foreseeing a future of forced submission subjected only to marital duties, at seventeen, Juana joined the barefoot Carmelites and a year later transferred to the convent of San Jerónimo in Mexico City. Her work began to circulate in and out of the Church. She soon acquired international acclaim for her exceptional poetry and writings. Shakespeare and Cervantes, contemporary writers, were the talk of Europe. Accused of pride in her fame, she was harassed by a Bishop in Mexico who forbid her use of her books. He accused the famous nun of arrogance. Sor Juana burned her library. Still in her prime, she took the vows of extreme poverty, volunteered to attend victims of the plague and died of the dread disease in 1695.

In the city of Puebla, at the foot of the "sleeping lady" volcano, a contemporary of Sor Juana was making her mark. "La China Poblana"[19] she was called, Puebla´s Chinese lady. Manila was not only the center of the Orient trade but the center of a cruel slave market. With cunning and violence, Chinese, Hindu and Polynesian women were captured and brought to the slave pens of Manila, often destined for men of wealth in distant parts of the world. "La China" is said to have been born a Princess in a Sultan´s harem on the banks of the Mekong river. She was a prize - regal and beautiful. Slated as a concubine for a ruthless Minister, destiny digressed her path to the home of a pious Catholic family in Puebla under whose tutelage she became devoted to the Church and good works. But it is her original mode of dress for which she is most remembered: the red and green sequined and beaded skirt worn by dancers in the "Mexican hat dance" is called a "China Poblana" costume. La China was buried on the grounds of a convent in Puebla in 1690 and is a witness to the oriental influence in Mexico.

> *Throughout the seventeenth century the sun was hibernating, hiding behind dark clouds, provoking storms and gusts of discontent both in the motherland and her American possessions.*

One catastrophe after another ended Spain´s dream of dominion in Europe and new conquests in North America. Spain´s power progressively diminished. Three weak Austrian kings, more intent on defending their inherited possessions in Europe than in resolving the crisis at home

---

19 Literal translation of the term "china poblana" is "a woman of the pueblo (town) who has slanted eyes"

and abroad, waged continuous war resulting in the loss of Holland and Austria. After a long attempt at unification, Portugal broke away. On the Iberian peninsula, draught caused crops to fail, hunger caused riots and uprisings. Three epidemics of the plague broke out in Europe during the century killing a million Spaniards. Wars further decimated the population and the expulsion of the Arabs early on took away 300,000 productive citizens. Villages were empty, many industries at a standstill in Spain.

To exacerbate Spain´s misfortunes, silver production in New Spain decreased dramatically. Silver had fueled the economic development of much of Europe for more than a hundred years. Spain´s wars as well as her lavish Court life were paid with Mexico and Peru´s silver and gold. As the Crown´s debts mounted, more silver was demanded and the Monarchy squeezed every cent out in taxes.

Now, one catastrophe after another also struck New Spain: Hard labor and devastating epidemics had reduced the native population to 75,000. The wind blew up dust over untilled lands parched by draught. A new disease, yellow fever, broke out in Veracruz. In Yucatán, the *Mayas*, who refused to be brought under the Spanish yoke, revolted and killed the Governor leaving the Viceroy meager defenses to put down the citizen uprisings in the Capital. The Indians in Oaxaca revolted, the French sacked Veracruz and the English pirate, Henry Morgan, burned and sacked the port of Panama, preventing the passage of Incan silver and gold. To protect Spanish Florida, the fort of Pensacola was built. To the north, the French had taken possession of a huge territory called Louisiana and the English had settled the territory of Virginia. As the century ended, a revolt by hungry citizens in 1692 nearly destroyed the Municipal Palace and the Palace of the Viceroy in the great square of the Capital of New Spain. Creoles, mestizos and Indians alike rioted in concert against the exorbitant prices of corn and other basics. The rigid apparatus of control upon which the society of New Spain was built began to show fissures.

In the jungles of New Spain, the old gods were laughing as the Sun God shown brighly on the English colonies to the north.

The English colonies were thriving with a growing mercantile trade protected by England´s Navy. Spanish fortifications and outposts in the Caribbean were poorly defended. The Dutch colony of New York and the Swedish settlement on the Delaware were closely allied to the English settlements. In 1643 the thirteen colonies, having paid off their debts to the capitalists who had financed their voyages, united in a Confederation As the seventeenth century progressed, young industries were started in the colonies of Rhode Island, New Jersey and Pennsylvania. Tobacco grown in Virginia, rice in Carolina and sugarcane in the West Indies were bringing huge revenues to the colonies.

As the sword had been the Spaniard´s arm, the musket was the protestant settler´s defense. The Indians of North America were for the most part nomads, followers of the buffalo, trappers and wood cutters. At first friendly, as their land was encroached upon, Indian attacks were repelled with firearms. Women shouldered guns next to their men and the colonies grew closer together in defense of the furious Indian raids. Methodically, the native population was almost totally eliminated. At first, indentured white servants had tilled the fields, but as they worked off their seven-year contract as servants bound to a master, more black field hands were needed. In 1689 Spain granted the lucrative slave contract to the English in an attempt to diminish their continuous harassment in the Caribbean.

In contrast to the Spanish conquerors, wives had accompanied the English settlers to the new world; they worked side by side with their husbands and passed on English traditions and morals to the next generation. But a child whose bloodlines were crossed between a white European and Indian or black was rejected as a "crossbreed." Towns grew as the mercantile trade became more profitable, attracting more and more white settlers. Hard work and discipline were the common code of ethics. Neat rows of wooden houses divided only by low picket fences multiplied around town squares. A simple, wooden church was the center of social life. Protestant zeal was as strong in the north as was Catholic in the south. In 1692 a group of hysterical young women were accused of witchcraft and burned at the stake in Salem, Massachusetts.

In 1682 an English astronomer, Edmund Halley, observed a comet, calculated its orbit and projected its return in 1757. In New Spain, a devout Indian convert observed the Torch of God lighting the sky and felt a surge of new hope.

The death of Charles II in 1700 ended the Austrian line in Spain and brought the French to the Spanish throne; the grandson of Louis XIV became Phillip V, the first Bourbon king.

CHAPTER VI

The Sun God threw off his gray mantle and came out in all his glory. in the XVIII century New Spain reached its moment of maximum splendor.

Something spontaneous was emerging from the ashes of *Tenochtitlán*, a sense of unity culled from totally disparate beliefs and cultures. The spiritual vacuum had been filled; devotion to a pantheon of saints and village patronesses was expressed in joyous *fiestas* where the old rites of death found a place in candy skulls and masks. More cognizant of the needs of their parishioners, local priests permitted ancient rituals to be incorporated into Christian festivals of worship. Religious fiestas were an outburst of fireworks and music and dance. In the Capital, where Viceroy and Archbishop continued their jousting over spiritual and secular power, each sponsored masked *fiestas* where all classes joined. The old languages were relegated to remote areas. A common language, common religion, shared commerce and new customs allowed the native Mexican to raise his head. Machines were introduced in textile mills and tanneries, small shops flourished in every town: the craftsman was an owner, salaries were paid to miners. In mid-century, workers in the tobacco factories demanded a 14-hour workday and although their protest was repudiated it created a feeling of union among workers.

Beautiful carved stone and brick buildings lined the streets of colonial towns and arcades graced tree-shaded town squares. Suitors strummed guitars beneath the balconies of their chosen lady. Families were closely knit, protected behind their walls. The great missionary drive in the XVII and XVIII centuries created towns of importance in the provinces where master builders constructed magnificent cathedrals and imposing municipal buildings and houses - in Puebla, Oaxaca, Taxco, Querétaro, Guanajuato, Guadalajara, Valladolid (today Morelia), Aguascalientes, Zacatecas, and other cities throughout Mexico. Crude roads paved with cobblestones all led to the Capital. Stagecoach service permitted people to move about more freely, broadening their horizon and sense of country. Mountains and blue skies that seemed to stretch to infinity dominated the landscape where church domes and bell towers rose high above the towns. But banditry was rampant and stagecoach passengers often arrived in the Capital in their underclothes, stripped of all possessions.

In the Capital, the first drainage system was constructed to carry off water which continuously flooded the streets. Master European painters fomented great native painting and sculpture. Magnificent works of art, painted by Mexican artists, began to supercede European masters and adorned the cathedrals and government palaces throughout colonial Mexico, religion the theme. Books were allowed to enter, and in 1788 the Metropolitan Library was established for the exclusive use of scholars, later to be opened to the public. Thanks to a Viceroy with vision, the archives of New Spain, mostly written by missionaries, and the few remaining Indian documents, were organized and stored in the Royal Palace in 1790. The professional class grew as academies and universities were founded. For the most part, life in the XVIII century was peaceful, its quiet monotony broken by feast days, market days, bullfights, cock fights, balls for the rich and noisy auctions of the goods imported from Spain and the Philippines.

The *haciendas* (country estates) belonged to the creoles who kept a tight rein on their Indian peasants. Like the English plantations in the north, the *haciendas* were an oasis in the countryside. These large extensions of land scattered through temperate to tropical climates fed the nation and exported a variety of products: coffee, sugar, beans, corn, wheat, rice and tobacco. (Note: Tobacco and syphilis, first exported from the Caribbean islands to Cadiz in 1493, were known as "the Indians' revenge".) *Charros*, the Mexican equivalent of cowboys, became a class of their own on the haciendas as cattle became more important; later, raising prize bulls required special skills. Feats of roping and horsemanship became trademarks of the *charros*. Saddles and trappings were adorned with silver as were their tight fitting black dress suits and hats. With the growth of the silver mines and large agricultural estates, family chapels took on a look of material splendor, baroque altars gleaming with gold leaf complemented by magnificent paintings and silver accouterments. Indian laborers on the haciendas were for the most part well fed and taken care of but in the silver mines, greed and cruelty was still unbridled.

In mid XVIII century, Father Junípero Serra started a drive north which was essential to establishing settlements in the northern territories. Missionaries accomplished what soldiers could not.

Friar Junípero Serra looked up at the *Sierra Gorda* mountains as he and his small band of barefoot Franciscans began their climb. He had arrived from Spain in 1749 and immediately decided that his task would be to build missions on and over the crest of the Sierra Gorda about 300 kilometers from the Capital. It was the natural boundary between the sedentary Indians of the central plateau and the nomadic hunter-tribes of the north. On the other side, it was reported, the territory comprised a dry, rugged landscape with scarce resources. No wonder the *Otomí* and *Chichimeca* were furiously attacking Spaniards who were driving cattle across their territory destroying their primitive farms. Friar Serra had a plan for evangelizing the Indians: he would choose sites with a source of water. Soon, the seeds they planted would produce crops and orchards. First, learn the language, feed the people, then start building the church. Indians were curious and would closely observe. Recruit them to help. With their help, they would also build adobe dwellings around the mission to offer housing. Be an example of what you teach.

Men of multiple skills, under the direction of missionaries, the Indian men were learning different trades: carpentry, plumbing, painting, stone sculpture, gilding and music. The women learned useful domestic habits. These dedicated friars of intelligence, goodness and morality were looked upon and respected as true fathers of the Indians. In Spanish they were referred to as "*padre*".

As missions were established farther into isolated territory, they became a compound which included an armed fort that protected them against Indian raids or other marauders. Enclosed vegetable and flower gardens and orchards added serenity and beauty to the compound. Chickens, goats and a few cows roamed the grounds. The life of the town was centered in the mission.

From the time of the Conquest all commerce with New Spain was closed to the outside world. Foreign ships could not anchor in her ports. All trade was regulated by the Council of Indies in Seville; commercial activity was restricted to the export of goods to and from Spain alone. The port of Cadiz, only, was authorized to receive and embark goods coming and going from the Americas. Its harbor was continually attacked by Barberry corsairs, the British fleet and other marauders. On the other side of the Atlantic, the Consul in Mexico, appointed by the Viceroy, was the designated magistrate in charge of all commerce. Under him, *Consulados*, merchant guilds, collected sales taxes, import taxes and the Royal Fifth. They conceded or sold commercial contracts to local merchants. As members of the elite *Consulado*, powerful wholesale merchants in the Capital enjoyed a monopoly on all goods that entered and left the territory. They were owners of the big stores, the importers and exporters at the large trade fairs in Acapulco and Veracruz as well as the livestock fairs in the provinces. The *repartimiento*, distribution of raw materials and manufactured goods, was in their hands. Money was a rare commodity as it all passed through these same hands. Trade within and between the provinces was regulated by merchants who "bought" permits from the local Consul. They collected the tax at the custom house located at the border of each provincial territory. In addition, the buyer paid a tax on the goods he bought. A *Corregidor* was the Viceroy´s head magistrate in the provincial administrative order. He received money from the merchants to buy Indian products which, in turn, they sold to the mining towns whose supply of products depended upon this "circuit." Indians paid for raw materials and such luxuries as textiles, oil, rice and flour with future goods they produced. This arbitrarily priced "credit" usually left the debtor short of the amount he owed. Ambulant vendors, barter in local markets, city fairs, cooperative and town regulated granaries, helped to supply local needs. This system of distribution, *repartimiento*. was the mechanism that kept products, including gold and silver, under tight control and circulation. Middlemen thrived, and graft, contraband and corruption was practiced at every commercial level.

Rural property was divided in two ways: communal lands and individual ownership. In pre-hispanic times, clans or towns worked agricultural parcels together, cultivating for the benefit of the community. This practice was reinstated by Spain under the term known as the *ejido* system: the land belonged to the Crown but individual parcels were on perpetual loan to the farm laborer and his family. Private rural property, evolved from the original *encomiendas*, developed into the large haciendas in the hands of the creoles and clergy. Real estate had become of prime interest to the Church. Rental of properties funded schools, hospitals and charitable works, the ecclesiastical elite, and religious works of art.

In addition to fine silverwork and native crafts, tobacco, leather goods and textiles were allowed to be traded among the provinces, after export quotas were met. Transplanted coffee from Africa was becoming a crop of importance in New Spain, and with the invention of the cotton gin, production of cotton grew rapidly. By the end of the century, New Spain´s dependence on the old world for sustenance was minimal. Asia provided all the riches they could afford and illegal trade with the islands was cheaper and closer.

The dulled jewels in the crown of Spain glowed with a new light when it was placed on the head of Charles III in 1759. He had sat on the throne of Italy and brought new vision to feudal rule.

When Charles III ascended the throne of Spain he faced the alarming news of the occupation of Quebec by the English. The Empire of Spain´s arch enemy was spread around the world, an Empire comprised of India, Australia, New Zealand and Canada. They were entrenched in the Caribbean; they were a thorn in the heel of Spain - Gibralter. His own American Empire was shaking. Rebellions were breaking out from New Spain to the tip of South America. Charles III had no recourse but to wage a series of wars against England to protect his Caribbean possessions. He could not get his galleons through those pirate-infested waters controlled by the English. In a nightmare come true, England stormed and occupied Havana and Manila, destabilizing colonial Spain. Astutely Charles offered eastern Florida, from the Bay of Pensacola north, in return for his prize islands. In order to allow his galleons to pass, England demanded a part of the silver cargo. In spite of the fact that they were at war, Charles struck a secret deal: ten percent of the cargo in return for unintercepted passage to Spain. In his agreement, the English King stated: "If this is known, I will deny it."

Why did England derive more goods and revenue from its American colonies than Spain with its vast dominions? Charles pondered: Cadiz was a thieves´ den, replete with a network of foreign agents linked to Mexico, Peru and the Philippines. Contraband and corruption were the grease of commerce. He had had to pay a large ransom to allow his silver and gold to cross the Atlantic. And his other goods? Indians, who composed sixty percent of the population of New Spain, cultivated the major part of the arable land. Why was their export of grains so poor? A wise former Minister of the Treasury had written: "Freedom is the root of commerce without which it cannot flower. The colonies are a great potential market for Spain herself. To achieve this state, their own commerce must grow." The colonists needed more purchasing power. Money! Why import leather and export expensive shoes when they could be manufactured in America? The English colonies produced quality manufactured goods; Boston and New York had thriving industries which produced revenue for the colonies which in turn became an important market for England. Industries had been prohibited in New Spain because they were considered competition for the market in Spain itself. Only crafts and the production of metals was allowed. New Spain exported its produce, paying a trifle to the farmer, leaving only sufficient for the local market. Well, the English colonies were a small territorial possession and self-government saved the Crown a lot of headaches. They were not viceroyalties that spread over a continent. King Charles pondered and took council. Lower taxes, increased manufacture and more effective methods of production, especially in the mines, should be studied, he concluded.

In 1765, Charles III dispatched José de Galvez to New Spain as a *visitador* (inspector). Galvez was astute, honest and qualified to do an exhaustive audit of the financial status of Spain´s prize possession. He was also empowered to take a census of the population and make a study of all enterprises in which the Crown´s subjects were engaged. No one was exempt! He was to report directly to the King.

With full authority of the King, Galvez and his elite entourage began to unravel the corrupt, illegal system of *repartimiento* bringing down on his head a legion of disgruntled middlemen. He set straight the justice system and diminished the power of the *Consulados* breaking the monopoly of the despotic merchants who controlled all trade. In the provinces, he restructured the custom houses and all systems of taxation. The Indians were permitted to freely buy and sell. A heavy mercantile tax set up a howl of "unfair!" but Galvez stood steadfast.

In Spain, King Charles opened eleven ports to commerce with his American possessions, breaking Cadiz´ monopoly. He soon permitted the Caribbean islands to trade directly with New Spain. A system of *intendencias*, administrative districts, was installed. An *Intendente* was a Spanish born administrator who was responsible to the Council of Indies, not the Viceroy.

Charles thought that by unifying the administrative and fiscal organization of New Spain, his problems with the colony would be solved. But his "enlightened reforms" did not take into account social transformation.

The wind wailed a long lament as it bent tall pines, scrubby oak trees and tropical palms in its furious path through the provinces where adobe missions closed their doors. Storms flooded schools, hospitals, orphanages, shelters and asylums.

In 1767, by order of Charles III, the Jesuits were expelled from New Spain. Rioting citizens hurled barrages of stones at government offices and the militia. In the town of San Luis de la Paz, thousands of Indian women formed a veritable wall of protest. In Guanajuato, the miners tried to hide their Jesuit teachers in the mines but were caught and hanged.

All aspects of life in New Spain were subordinated to religion. Only the rich could send their sons to Spain to be educated in secular universities. Education was in the hands of the Church, influencing character, conduct and ideas. Nuns were in charge of elementary education, teaching children to read and write, but it was the Jesuits who were considered the true educators. Zealous, well-educated Jesuit priests of "The Company of Jesus" were proponents of a liberal philosophy. They taught against the abuses of sovereigns and encouraged discussion. With their full approval, studious creoles and mestizos smuggled in French books which dealt with the new liberal ideas gestating in

Europe. Secretly, the books of Rousseau and Voltaire were passed on, creating a new intellectual focus and a new perspective of colonial Spain. Voltaire claimed that the seeking spirit (the God within, not without), built civilization and enriched human life. Fanaticism and orthodoxy were enemies of civilization. Accused of sedition by the Spanish monarch, the Jesuits were expelled from all his American possessions, the Philippines and Spain, itself.

> *Draught dried the blossoms in the orange groves and waves crashed on the California coast The Jesuits had left.*

Fast on their heels Franciscans and a few Dominicans friars were assigned to the mission settlements. After friar Junípero Serra had established missions in the mountains of the Sierra Gorda, he and his barefoot band of Franciscans walked down from the craggy heights of central Mexico to traverse the hot, spiny northern territories. They established a mission in San Antonio, then headed west to El Paso and San Diego. To this day Father Serra is remembered at the mission of San Juan de Capistrano in southern California.

Mission settlements and outposts were built in Our Lady of Angels, Santa Barbara, Monterrey Bay and San José. A mild climate, fertile soil and ample water gave rise to a growing economy which became the bloodline of the Californias. Moving farther north, Father Serra discovered a beautiful, expansive bay and peninsula which he named the "Golden Gate". The natives were peaceful and receptive. Reporting the extraordinary site to the Viceroy, an expedition was sent to build a fort and settlement around the small mission of San Francisco. In 1776 the mission of

Santa Clara was founded. Fear, lest the English or Russians obtain the Pacific territories, hastened the mission link of 21 settlements and forts along the California coast as far north as Oregon. By necessity the settlements were self-sustaining. Priests had little contact with their superiors in the Capital whose superiors were in Rome. Recognizing the formidable power of the Church, Charles III secular-ized the local parish churches, separating them from the religious Orders.

Since 1775 there were words in the wind, English words, whispered words that spoke of battle: Lexington and Concord. The word Independence resonated loudly.

Veracruz was rife with rumor: it was said that the colonists in Boston had poured hot tea on the head of the English tax collector. The words continued to be heard, resonating louder.... Bunker Hill, Philadelphia ... In 1776 the English Colonists had issued a Declaration of Inde-pendence! England had sent over seasoned Regiments and 29,000 German mercenaries backed by her navy. Charles III had again declared war on England. Spanish ships were secretly leaving Cuba with arms and money for the rebel-lious English colonists.... The French fleet had entered Chesapeake Bay to assist General Washington, under siege. A battle in Yorktown was won! In 1783 *England lost her thirteen colonies!*

In the Viceroy´s court, heads met: rumors of conspira-cies by disgruntled creoles must not be permitted to fester! Galvez lost no time in instituting the draft. Hitherto, the only soldiers were the King´s Royal forces, thinly spread through the provinces. Now, at Galvez´ command, all men, of all castes, from sixteen to forty had to register in the militia lists. Negro and mulato laborers were pressed into service to fortify Veracruz. Five thousand workers built the fort of San Juan de Ulua,, a formidable stone fortress visible from all parts of the bay. Spain´s old enemy, England, might decide to move south! Military units were dispatched to the outposts in the northern territories and Galvez headed a military expedition that subdued the Indians of Sonora.

José Galvez was awarded the title of "Marqués de la Sonora" and in 1785 was named Universal Secretary of the Indies in Spain. His son became a Viceroy and a nephew became Governor of the Louisiana Territory. He had followed in his uncle´s footsteps, personally accompanying an expedition to Texas giving name to the port of Galveston.

1793: Don Antonio de Alba y Ramirez had the gracious manner and practical character of his Spanish father and the stoic endurance and hidden fears of his mestiza mother. He had worked hard since he was a boy; starting with a few head of cattle, he had invested every penny to increase his herd and land. His sons had spurred the business of meat and hides. The new tannery held great promise. He now dedicated his time to his avocations: raising fighting bulls and fighting cocks. A year ago, his oldest son had left for Spain to take advantage of family connections to set up a business in the export of leather goods. The boy´s head seemed filled more with political ideas than business! Well, he had sent him to that liberal college in San Miguel el Grande. Although the Jesuits were long gone, their colleges had produced a new breed of young men.

"Liberals" they were called, but smart. The boy would bring home good news.

As Don Antonio rode into San Miguel to meet the stage coach bringing home his son, his own mind was filled with confusing thoughts. That new country up there, calling itself the United States of America, was causing havoc: like a rabbit warren, its "Bill of Rights" bored underground and popped up at every discussion causing division among friends and family. Only the presence of the Royalist forces in San Miguel prevented open rebellion. His younger son had vehemently defended the ideas of a man named Thomas Jefferson. He should be thinking about the new Royal School of Mines just opened in the Capital. The nearby mines of Guanajuato needed capable men. Mining investments could be a future goal. Don Antonio shook his head.

In a festive mood, the family gathered around their long table to hear young Tonio tell of his travels. "They´re frightened, I tell you. And King Charles is going to tighten the noose on us," the young man expounded. "I was in Seville last June when the news arrived from France. A mob invaded the Tuileries in Paris and imprisoned the royal family. They stormed the Bastille then executed Louis XVI and soon after, Queen Marie Antoinette". He ran his hand across his throat. "The guillotine!"

CHAPTER VII

The X1X century was issued in with shock waves that set nerves on edge throughout Europe. Revolution was in the air. "The King is dead, long live the Republic" was the cry in France.

In Paris, a young artillery officer had witnessed the executions of Louis XV1 and Antoinette in 1793. Napoleon Bonaparte´s zeal for the Revolution and scorn for the weakness of the French King destined him to an immortal place in history. Soon, Europe staggered as the Captain was raised to General and engaged one country after another in battle.

The march of Napoleon was unprecedented in military history: Lodi, Milan, Arcol, Rivoli, Vienna. Austria fell. Rome, Geneva, Bern, Malta. The Kingdom of Naples fell. Across the Mediterranean, the Turks were defeated and Cairo occupied. As the XIX century dawned, Napoleon was elected First Consul of the French Republic. Austria and Italy were his. After 700 years the Holy Roman Empire ceased to be. Napoleon´s star was in ascendance - Savior of the Republic, Master of Europe. In 1804 Napoleon, himself, placed the crown of France upon his head in the presence of the Pope in Paris. He was hailed Emperor! In 1805 he was again crowned in Milan Cathedral. Battles raged in Austerlitz, Jena, Bavaria, Berlin. England was the thorn. Seizure of England´s merchant ships and closure of all continental ports to British vessels caused a Lion´s roar to reverberate throughout the British Isles. Napoleon´s brothers, Joseph, Louis and Jerome Bonaparte ascended the thrones of Italy, Holland and Westphalia. Napoleon dissolved the Tribunate in France. His star had reached its zenith. The power of an absolute sovereign was now his.

1808: Rebellions in Spain and a dispute over the Crown between Carlos IV, a weak king who had been forced to abdicate by his son, Fernando VII, opened the way for Napoleon to invade Spain. It was the moment to seize the throne in Madrid. On the pretext of opening a breach to Portugal, England´s ally and Spain´s enemy, he accomplished his goal, brought his brother Joseph from Italy and crowned him King of Spain.

When the news arrived in Mexico, the populace was in shock. The King was gone! Kidnapped by Napoleon and spirited off to Paris in forced exile while Napoleon´s brother, Joseph, sat on the throne of Spain. In the Palace on the great square in Mexico, the Viceroy breathed heavily and pondered his predicament. In whose name was he governing? To whom should he report? Members of the *Cabildo* (Municipal Government) had proposed that he form a ruling *Junta* (assembly) with the city governors and local authorities as delegates to rule until Fernando VII was restored to the throne. It seemed a reasonable solution; a Central Assembly in Spain had already convened. The Viceroy called an emergency meeting of his top officials. What? A ruling assembly with the creoles in charge – never! In a rapid coup, the elite cadre of top peninsular officials arrested the Viceroy, accused him of treason and put him in jail. They declared themselves the Ruling Council. As soon as word went out of the coup by the peninsulares, rebellions began to break out throughout the country. The peninsulares quickly sent to Cuba for reinforcements for the Royalist Army. Most of the soldiers in the Royalist Army were mestizos drafted or pressed into service; their officers were creoles, a jealous, often mutinous lot whose loyalty leaned more toward New Spain than Mother Spain.

Through the generations the creoles had become a class unto themselves, marrying among themselves to maintain their social advantages and family patrimony. They were the investors in the mines, the owners of stores and factories, the occupants of the large houses on the town squares. They were the large landholders. They supported the Church; they gave the money that built Cathedrals and hospitals, patronized orphanages and convents and donated funds for civic projects. They were an oligarchy. Some were addressed by titles handed down from the conquerors and *encomenderos* or acquired titles through marriage to descendents of old Spanish nobility. Some titles were bought and some were considered questionable. They entertained lavishly and their ladies wore brocades and fine silk from China. Many spoke French, the language associated with "culture".

They were the godparents of each others´ children. Through these family alliances and close relationship with the hierarchy of the Church, occasionally a creole entered the inner sanctum of the Court or might be granted a plumb regional position. But there was a limit to their aspirations: there was always a peninsular, a man born in Spain, above them, in the administrative line, in the fiscal field, in the courts, in the military and in the Church.

As the XIX century dawned in Spanish America, the population of New Spain was approximately 6,000,000. Roughly 40,000 were *peninsulares*, 1,000,000 *criollos*, 1,500,000 *mestizos* and 3,500,000 Indians, only slightly larger than the Indian population at the time of the conquest, three centuries earlier.

The Church dominated all segments of colonial society. Life was regulated by bells: the bells of the great cathedrals and parochial churches awakened the citizens at 5:00 in the morning; at 12:00 noon the angelus was rung, invoking prayers and setting the time to eat and rest. After the siesta, at 3:00 in the afternoon, the bells called people to Mass in remembrance of the death of Christ. At sundown, the evening angelus again invoked prayer; at 8:00 the bells rang for fifteen minutes and curfew was tolled from 9:00 to 10:00. Bells announced the arrival of the mail boat from Spain and the arrival of the Nao de la China in Acapulco. They tolled 100 times to announce the death of a Viceroy and clanged lugubriously after an earthquake or other disaster. Usually solemn, sometimes joyful, each bell had a special "voice" and personality. They were baptized and named by the patron or donor who would throw in a piece of family jewelry to add a personal touch to the metal. The Church ruled life and the parochial priest was God´s arbiter.

Miguel Hidalgo y Costilla was a creole,[20] the son of a wealthy Spaniard who was the overseer of a large hacienda. Gifted with a bright intellect, he had only three courses of study open to him: Philosophy, Theology or Law. Among the liberal professionals, lawyers abounded, but the intellectuals were men of the Church. A devout Christian, Hidalgo pursued an ecclesiastical course. He studied for the priesthood and became an avid student of Church history. Early on, doubts flickered on the altar of his conscience: he questioned the dogma of the Church, the proclamation of Divine Right, the power of the Inquisition, the sanctity of corrupt Popes; Cannon Law itself. Had Voltaire not said that the seeking spirit, the God within, not without, built civilization and enriched human life? Had he not said that fanaticism and orthodoxy were enemies of civilization? As a teacher of theology, more and more Hidalgo relied on his own Christian sentiments arousing the ire of the Inquisition. At age 45, he closed his books and resigned as Rector of the College of San Nicolás in the city of Valladolid (a Jesuit bastion) and became the devoted parish priest of the small town of Dolores in the province of Guanajuato. He was soon fluent in several Indian tongues and became a champion of "his" people. Also a man of worldly tastes, he enjoyed good food, good wine, card-playing and the company of women and musicians. He made known his liberal political views from the pulpit.

Since Napoleon´s invasion of Spain, in 1808, the word "Independence" had risen from a whisper to a loud clamor

---

20 Creole (criollo) in those days also meant a person of mixed blood, but not necessarily of pure Spanish parentage, who was born and raised in America.

in the Spanish colonies. Conspiracies flared and were put down by Royalist forces, only to flare again. In Spain itself, continuous war raged the length and breadth of the peninsula to drive out Napoleon´s invaders. Anticipating the return of Fernando VII, a Supreme Junta convened in Cadiz and approved a liberal constitution which established a constitutional monarchy. In New Spain, the group of *peninsulares* who had seized the rein of government reluctantly accepted the authority of the Cadiz Junta which ruled in the name of the absent King..

A short distance from Dolores, in the town of San Miguel el Grande, a conspiracy had been gestating in the barracks of the Royalist garrison.led by Captain Ignacio Allende. Also a creole, Allende felt the stigma of a second class citizen, never able to aspire to the high rank of a peninsular nor have a voice in the government of his own country. This was his land, not Spain! While his guests danced to the lively airs of the polka in his parlor in plain sight of the main square, Allende and fellow conspirators met in a back room and secretly plotted their uprising. They would take over the Ruling Council in the Capital. Equality and liberty to rule themselves was their goal! Word of the conspiracy reached the ears of the Spanish magistrate (Corregidor) in Querétaro and his wife, Doña Josefa, who became a key player. Soon, Hidalgo joined the conspirators. Knowing his popularity and leadership, Allende asked the priest to head the uprising: with a priest at the head, they could not be accused of being anti-Church. Reluctantly, Hidalgo, now 56, agreed to raise an army and march to San Miguel where he would join Allende´s forces and march on, gathering an army en route to the Capital. It would be a swift revolt.

A warm, dense air blew down from the cloud shrouded Sierra Madre picking up the perfume of forbidden wine which was fermenting in the oak vats of father Miguel Hidalgo´s vineyards near the town of Dolores.

Allende and Hidalgo were going over the plan of action in Hidalgo´s house when an exhausted rider brought word from Doña Josefa in Querétaro that the plot had been discovered. Captain Ignacio Allende knew they must act quickly. The time was now! Riding at full gallop he left to prepare his Royalist troops in the barracks in San Miguel. Hidalgo would assemble a troop and meet him there next morning.

Pacing up and down in the atrium of his church early the morning of September 16, 1810, Miguel Hidalgo´s mind churned with contradicting thoughts: son of a wealthy family, he knew the restrictions that his creole class suffered, but more, he sympathized with his Indian parishioners. Freed from the yoke of servitude – and educated - his Indians would develop into a new class, equal members of a free society. To break with Spain completely, however, was not his intention. It was the land of his fathers. But to have constitutional freedom to govern themselves was imperative! Fernando VII must be restored to the throne as a constitutional monarch. Napoleon had not only imprisoned the King, he had imprisoned the Pope! He was the anti-Christ! Tinges of a Holy War assuaged Hidalgo´s priestly conscience.

Resolutely, father Hidalgo rang the bells with all his strength, calling his people to morning Mass. The church was soon full. He began his harangue, calling for an uprising in defense of the legitimate King of Spain, in defense of the Virgin of Guadalupe, in defense of a voice in government. "Viva Fernando VII! Viva the Virgin of Guadalupe! Death to the bad government!" was the original cry that morning of September 16, 1810.

Hidalgo´s cry of liberty discharged a geyser of rancor and hatred, repressed for centuries. He threw open the prison doors, releasing prisoners who joined the multitude of peasants armed with *machetes* and iron bars and sticks and stones and spades. They advanced on San Miguel like an avalanche, pausing in the village of Atotonilco to take down a canvas of the Virgin of Guadalupe which they mounted and bore on high as their standard. "Death to the gachupines!" (Spaniards) became their cry as they burned and sacked and destroyed Spanish property. In San Miguel, seeing the raging wave approach, Captain Allende crammed Spaniards into the empty Jesuit school to save their lives. Hidalgo marched on to the rich mining town of Guanajuato where Allende joined him. Seeing Hidalgo´s inability to control the hordes, he controlled his own troops. The priest stood by while they killed and pillaged! The massacre of Spaniards who had taken refuge in the Alhondiga, a stone storage house atop a hill, became the battle cry of the avenging Royalist troops. But the Virgin had become the symbol of the insurrection, giving cohesion to the growing popular movement.

In a month the rebel forces had swelled to 50,000 and headed for the Capital where a new Viceroy had been installed. On the outskirts they defeated the Royalists, leaving the road to victory open.

> *Darkness fell over the city like the black curtains of the funeral cars. The Capital was enveloped in fearful silence. Peninsulares hid their money and their jewels and ladies rushed out in the night to hide in convents as barricades were hastily erected to protect the city. Like a rush of wind, the word spread: the rebels were coming! The viceroy had the Spanish virgin of "los Remedios", patron saint of Spain, brought from her shrine and placed in the Cathedral where he commissioned her "Captain General of all Spanish forces in the Americas."*

On the battlefield near the city, the ragged, victorious insurgent troops awaited orders. Shouts went up: "Death to the gachupines !" "Viva the Virgin of Guadalupe!" Hidalgo did not move. Suddenly, on the verge of victory, he gave orders to turn northeast – retreat! Perhaps he was fearful of the violence and pillage and disorder an attack on the Capital would provoke. As Hidalgo led his army back toward Guanajuato, thousands deserted including creoles who believed in his cause. Why? Why did Hidalgo turn back when the Capital was within their sight! Historians have yet to agree on the cause.[21]

Without slowing his march, Hidalgo established his headquarters at Guadalajara where he tried to organize a government and succeeded in raising another army. Victims of a poorly planned military tactic, his army was ambushed, cut down and dispersed by Royalist troops

The metamorphosis from priest to revolutionary, par-

---

21 Hidalgo explained it in a letter written from Celaya on November 18: The Insurgents had lost a lot of ammunition, many people had defected and the armies of Felix Calleja and Manuel Flon were approaching.

ticipant in violent bloodshed and plunder for which he was responsible, must have weighed heavily on Hidalgo´s priestly conscience. He had promised the return of ancestral lands to the Indians; he had encouraged them to fight. But the revolution had degenerated into anarchy. Mexico was not ready for independence.

Hidalgo endured his imprisonment without complaint. Silently, he faced expulsion from the Catholic Church. Ten months after the "*Grito de Hidalgo*", his call to arms that fateful morning of September 16, 1810, the heads of Hidalgo, Allende, Jimenez and Aldama hung in cages from the four corners of the Alhondiga in Guanajuato where the Spaniards had been massacred.

The banner of liberty torn from Hidalgo was taken up by another priest, José María Morelos. Hidalgo had been his teacher at the Jesuit college in Valladolid. A man of high principle, courage and discipline, Morelos saw the struggle for independence as a mission. His ideals and political astuteness were transcendental in the formation of Mexico as a nation. A mestizo of humble origin and a parish priest, Morelos had witnessed the ethnic stigma and misery of the Indians and those known as "castes", the varied mixtures of white, Indian and blacks. Hidalgo had fanned a class war; Morelos wanted to reconcile all classes. Liberty and equality went hand in hand. He fought the Spaniards not because they were Spanish but because they were the enemies of liberty. Morelos formed a well-trained, offensive army of disciplined soldiers whose purpose in fighting was one: absolute independence from Spain. Looting and destruction of property were prohibited.

The battle of Cuautla is one of the most extraordinary feats of this extraordinary leader. Continually pursued and harassed by the Royalist army, in 1812 Morelos and his troops took refuge in the unfortified town of Cuautla, in the State which today bears his name. Exhausted soldiers fell asleep on the pews and floor of the church while others were given haven in the houses of the townspeople. In the morning, it was clear they were surrounded. Soon, they were under siege by a strong, Royalist army. Arriving at full gallop, an assemblage of well-saddled horsemen converged in the town plaza where a throng of civilians, every man woman and child fit to do manual work, was feverishly building barricades. The leader approached a soldier and said, "Advise General Morelos that we are twenty well-armed volunteers at his disposition." Father and son, jefe and servant, ranchers, Indian field hands, creoles, mestizos, castes fought side by side in defense of Cuautla. "The color of the face does not change the color of the heart", Morelos is quoted. "We are all Americans." Morelos bravery and resolute stand inspired daring forays into the Royalists camps to weaken their positions. But in the heat of an intense barrage, the outnumbered defenders of the barricade suddenly ran back wildly, dispersing, jumping over bodies. A ragged young boy noticed a cannon ready to be fired. He picked up a burning stick and fired! In a panic, the advancing Royalists retreated. The name of the boy hero, Narciso Mendoza, is noted in the annals of Mexican history. After sixty-three days, Morelos´ starving army broke the siege.

Morelos escaped and reassembled his scattered troops, moving on to capture Oaxaca and lay siege to the port of

Acapulco. He soon controlled the south and was recognized as Supreme Commander of the Insurgent forces. In 1813 he convoked a Congress which issued a "Declaration of Independence" and ratified a Constitution which gave legal basis to the war. Abolition of slavery (decreed earlier by Hidalgo), abolition of designation by ethnic caste, abolition of Church and Army privileges, including compulsory tithes, equal rights for all citizens and a just distribution of land were sketched in this first constitution. Morelos´ dream of a new social and economic order would be the basis for reform for the next century.

Destiny led Morelos into a trap: heading northeast to Valladolid (later to be named "Morelia" in his honor) he faced a Royalist bastion. Valladolid, the city where he was born and had been a student of Hidalgo, was doomed to turn the tide in favor of the Royalists. Defeated and weakened, Morelos was soon captured. He was taken in chains to Mexico City. There the Inquisition decried him a "heretic" and refused him last rites as he faced a firing squad. Morelos was executed in 1815.

Across the ocean, Napoleon´s star had sunk low on the horizon. After planting the banner of the French Republic across three quarters of Europe, in 1812 his Grand Army invaded Russia with 550,000 troops; only 20,000 staggered back with him to Paris. Unable to rally his former military might, Napoleon abdicated in 1814 and was banished to the island of Elba. He escaped to raise another army, only to face the English General, Wellington. Wellington had crossed through Portugal to Spain where he joined the rebel Spanish army in chasing the French invaders back across the Pyrenees into France. It is said that the last battle is the only battle that counts. Napoleon was defeated by Wellington at Waterloo in 1815.

Fernando VII, the weak King of the Bourbon line, was rescued from France and restored to the Spanish throne.

Fernando's first act was to exercise his "divine right" by arresting the Assembly in Cadiz and declaring the new constitution null and void. The Monarchy was in turmoil and New Spain in a frenzy. Fernando paced: Morelos had laid siege to Acapulco immobilizing his Philippine galleon. British ships were anchored in Veracruz supplying the rebels and taking out cargos of silver! Word had reached him that wealthy miners had joined the insurgent cause providing the rebels with capital and buying arms abroad. The United States was fanning the cause, also supplying arms. Only a trickle of grains and tobacco and textiles and leather goods were reaching Spain. The economy was in chaos! Fernando sent Spanish troops across the ocean and ordered Spanish forces from Cuba to put down the insurrection at all cost., too many creoles and mestizos were deserting the Royalist troops in New Spain. To top it off, like the plague, independent movements were gaining momentum up and down South America. Death to the traitors!

In New Spain, the Viceroy, now restored to full powers, thought the root of the insurrection had been severed; instead, new shoots had sprouted. Guerrilla war cropped up in one province after another. Bandits, led by provincial chieftains, were descending upon rich towns murdering and plundering at will. Only lack of centralized rebel leadership kept the Spanish in control.[22]

In the following six years the flame of independence became sparks ignited by the guerrilla chieftains whose troops hid in the mountains. Most of Morelos´ leaders were killed or imprisoned. By 1820, only two of his generals were alive: Vicente Guerrero and Guadalupe Victoria. The dry, blood-soaked soil was ravaged by ten years of war. Recruits deserted rather than give up their life for a futile cause. Independence hung by a thread.

---

22 During the eleven years of the War of Independence, the Spanish Viceroy remained in power and governed.

CHAPTER VIII

The great bell of the Cathedral, 15 tons of metal three meters high, began to ring incessantly at midnight. Had the bell-ringers gone crazy? Half-clothed people rushed into the street. The bells kept ringing. Puffing, the Bishop himself climbed to the belfry only to see a cat scampering away. No one was there!

The next morning, the boat from Spain arrived bringing momentous news: Fernando had been forced by his generals to accept the Cadiz Constitution and rule as a Constitutional Monarch. The Royalists were shaken to their roots. New vigor spurred the independent movement.

For the high clerical, military and creole classes, the Cadiz Constitution spelled doom to their status quo. Since mid XVIII century, the Bourbon kings had been chipping away at Church privileges. Now the liberal Congress in Cadiz had approved abolition of the Inquisition, confiscation of Church property, secular education, freedom of the press, equality of creoles and the worst ...it had placed the Church and Army under civil authority. Gone their immunity! The creole oligarchy saw the approaching spread of liberalism as a wave that would wash away their privileged position. Only absolute separation from the Spanish Monarchy could preserve their status quo. Removal from Spanish law was the answer.

Agustin Iturbide, who had defeated Morelos at Valladolid, was a Royalist general and a gifted strategist of arrogant and amibitious character. Like Hidalgo, Allende and Morelos, he had been educated at the Jesuit college of San Nicolás in Valladolid. And like Hidalgo, he was a creole. Both were sons of wealthy *peninsulares*, one bent on destroying the fortunes and properties of their class and fomenting hatred of the Europeans (death to the gachupines!), the other convinced that Hidalgo´s hordes were a plague on the land.

By 1820, Iturbide knew that the cry for independence would not die out. He viewed the new Constitutional Monarchy as an opportunity to negotiate peace. Backed by the privileged class, he was encouraged to find a formula for establishing an Independent Empire, better by far than a Republic which a group of zealous creoles, with eyes on the United States, were advocating in loud terms. An independent Mexican Empire was a feasible basis for peace.

Iturbide held a secret meeting with General Guerrero, the last rebel general still engaged in battle. After short deliberation, Iturbide and Guerrero embraced. They were weary of war. They both laid down their arms and issued a joint decree, known as the Accord of the Three Guarantees: (1) Independence from Spain (2) Government by a constitutional monarchy (the monarch to be sent by Fernando VII) (3) Full support of the Roman Catholic Church as the sole religion of the nation and equality of creoles. In essence it guaranteed independence, a constitutional monarchy and continued privileges, acceptable terms for Royalists and Federalists. Had not Napoleon succeeded in melding these same opposing forces into an Empire? In August, 1821, the 62rd and last Viceroy, Juan O.Donojú, landed in Veracruz A liberal, he ratified the Accord with the authority granted him by the King.

On September 27, 1821, the roof-tops, the trees, the streets were lined with cheering crowds who showered flowers in the path of the great Army of the Three Guarantees (El Ejército Trigarante). Cries of "Viva el Libertador!" resonated as Agustin Iturbide, mounted on a magnificent black horse, entered the great square where exactly three hundred years before Moctezuma had received Cortés. Sixty thousand soldiers paraded together, Royalists and Insurgents under the same banner, brothers united under a new flag. There it was, waving over the Palace: green for independence, white for the purity of religion and red for union with Spain. In the center an eagle sat upon a cactus with a snake clasped in its beak, honoring the Aztec Empire. To honor the new Empire, the eagle wore a crown. Jubilation and joy filled every heart - creole, mestizo, caste and Indian. Mexico was independent. Mexico was free|

Spain´s protest was immediate and loud. Fernando VII refused to recognize the loss of his prime domain, refused to send Mexico a monarch. The Vatican cancelled its recognition of the traditional civil rights of the Crown. What was Independence without a government? A provisional assembñy was hastily called, succeeded by an elected Congress. After furious debate, the Congress named Iturbide Emperor.

On July 21, 1822, Iturbide I was crowned Emperor of Mexico with all the pomp and ceremony a coronation merited. The Cathedral was resplendent and the bells joyously tolled the unprecedented event. But, like a theatrical prop, the Crown placed on Iturbide´s head, had neither history nor tradition.

It is said that the conquest of Mexico was made by the Indians (Cortes´ allies) and the Independence was made by the Spaniards.

The Mexican Empire was short lived. The seeds of anarchy were already planted.

In the chasm between the Monarchists and Federalists, differences of opinion on how the government should be organized tore the Congress apart. Just as Cortes had been faced with the question of how to administer the enormous Empire he had conquered, the Congress of this new Empire had to resolve how it would govern itself. The Monarchists, primarily large landholders, advocated all decisions and affairs of State to be determined by a central government. The Federalists, the merchant and professional middle class, advocated ample autonomy for each state. In spite of his pressure on members of Congress, Iturbide was unable to sway the majority to his way of thinking. In an authoritarian move, he suppressed freedom of the press and engaged Congress in open conflict. Passions ran high. In a rash, despotic decision, Iturbide dissolved the Congress.

The moment was ripe for an uprising. A brash young Royalist officer, Antonio Lopez de Santa Anna, who had supported Iturbide, turned against him. Quartered in the last Spanish bastion, the fortress of San Juan Ulua in Veracruz, this charismatic, creole Royalist defected to the Federalists and demanded reinstatement of the Congress. The revolt caught fire. Rapidly reassembling an army with liberal Royalists, Santa Anna marched toward the Capital. Iturbide was forced to abdicate and accepted exile in Europe. The Congress granted him a life pension and removed the Imperial Crown from the flag and coat of arms. The very man who had saved Mexico from anarchy now left the newborn country on the brink of becoming a nation divided.

A year later, in 1823, Iturbide returned, was arrested and faced a firing squad. Historians claim that unbeknownst to him, the reinstated Congress forbade his return. The execution of Iturbide raised passionate indignation and widened the chasm between the opposing groups.

In view of the seeming insoluble conflicts of interest, Guatemala separated from Mexico and together with its sister "Captaincies" decided to form their own Central American Federation. Mayan Chiapas broke away from Guatemala and continued to be annexed to Mexico.[23]

Recognizing its urgent need for unity, in 1822 a new Congress was convoked which drafted a constitution modeled on the constitution of the United States and the liberal constitution of Cadiz. The provinces of New Spain were divided into twenty states and four territories. The government was divided into three branches: Executive (to

---

23 When the territorial borders were being determined in 1824, Mexico appropriated the Soconusco, a portion of Guatemala, claiming it belonged to Chiapas.

be headed by an elected President), Legislative (with two chambers, Congress and Senate) and Judicial (to be headed by a Supreme Court). Although the Constitution did not contain a single article that guaranteed the rights of the individual, it did declare all citizens equal under the law.

In 1824, Congress ratified the new constitution. Mexico was decreed a free and independent Republic, constituted with the name of the United States of Mexico.

The constitutional guarantee of equality was almost impossible to apply. The creoles substituted the Spanish and the Church gained greater power and wealth. The Indian continued to be subject to arbitrary judgment. In his political essay on Mexico, Alexander Von Humboldt (the great botanist who traveled extensively through Mexico in 1804) stated that New Spain was a country of unequals where the color of a man´s skin decided his rank in society. He observed that a white man who rode a nag barefoot considered himself of noble blood. "Nowhere is there a more frightful distribution of fortunes, cultivation of land and discrimination of population," Humboldt wrote.

Mexico´s birth was long and painful. The social and economic problems which had dragged along, unresolved for three hundred years of colonial rule, now overwhelmed the experiment with democracy. Class divisions, illiteracy, a disperse population, isolation from contact and trade with other nations and above all, lack of experience in governing, left the organization and administration of the newborn country in the hands of an inexperienced few, a few who were continually at war with each other. Unlike its neighbor to the north, Mexico had not been prepared for independence, had not experienced self-rule, had not engaged in free trade. It was a culture bred in central authority, bred upon dependency, hermetically sealed off from the world outside of Spain. Passions ran high; federalism threatened to overturn the institutions, traditions and habits of centuries. New Spain had been the only true extension in the Americas of the mother country. It was not a colony, its people were subjects of Spain. Now the orphan had to fend for itself, make its own decisions. Though the cry of "liberty" was authentic, necessary and irreversible, few really understood what the word implied. The general belief in the fabled wealth of Mexico was almost a dogma among the governing class. All they had to do was exploit their great national wealth to raise them from the morass of eleven years of pain and conflict. Like the tribe of *Mexicas* who had seen the eagle in the lake, they saw a future of wealth and prestige. A few realists saw the truth: silver mines, fuel of New Spain´s economy, abandoned or flooded, agriculture destroyed and incipient industries unattended. A few believed that new industry was the answer. The industrial revolution was creating great wealth in Europe and the United States. Mexico was barely emerging from a feudal state; an industrialized Mexico would rise to world status, would build a solid economy. But Mexico was a country with no long, navigable rivers, few roads, no railroads, immense, arid extensions in the north and jungles in the south, two oceans divided by prodigious mountains which had to be crossed. Its citizens were isolated from each other, its major cities cut off from the Capital nurturing provincial pride and traditions. Loyalty to the Spanish crown had held New Spain together. Now that mortar had crumbled. The new nation had no machinery, no fuel.... and no money. Mexico was bankrupt. Bankrupt with a territorial extension to the north that took in one third of future continental United States and to the south as far as Guatemala, territories not yet defined by cartographers, territories that would soon have to be defended. Its true dominions and resources were only dimly perceived. The branch that was torn from the trunk would nearly wither many times before it could begin to take root.

CHAPTER IX

MEXICO

From the outset, the United States had furnished the insurgents with arms, eager to be rid of Spain on its southern border. The moment Iturbide was crowned, the United States hastened to recognize Mexico´s independence. The presence of the English in the north and the Spanish, French and Dutch in the Caribbean was still considered a threat to the fast-growing Republic. In 1823, President James Monroe presented his famous document to Congress to be known as the "Monroe Doctrine". In essence it stated that any European intervention in the affairs of a government in the Americas, which had declared its independence and had been recognized by the United States, would be considered a threat to the security of the United States. It did not offer defense of the new independent Latin American nations but implied a determination by the United States to protect itself, and those around it, from European expansion.

Once the Constitution was approved and ratified, the new Mexican Congress called for presidential elections. Guadalupe Victoria, Morelos´ loyal General who had helped to keep the flame of Independence burning, was elected and installed as the first President. He was the only one until mid-century who succeeded in serving his full term.

Secret societies had penetrated Mexico since the time of the Jesuits, but by Independence Masonic lodges were a political force. They are believed to have been brought over by Spanish military officers: the fact that Generals Ignacio Allende and Vicente Guerrero were Masons tends to confirm this theory. In origin, masons had grouped together in European trade guilds. They were actual stone masons who bonded in "brotherhoods" to protect architectural secrets from other builders and to provide. mutual assistance. In Mexico, the Centralists were known as *escoseses*, Scottish-Rite masons, and the Federalists as *yorkinos*, York-Rite masons. In secret meetings, conspiracies and strategies were plotted. Masonic lodges would have a powerful influence in the political life of Mexico.[24]

Hastening to establish relations, the United States sent a representative to Mexico in 1822. He was received with misgivings: Mexico feared territorial expansion was the real interest of its powerful northern neighbor. Joel Poinsett, the first United States Minister and a Grand Master of free masonry, was to prove their suspicions correct. A tactless,

---

24 Today the Masonic emblem can be seen on the door of the entrance to the President´s office in the National Palace as well as other official offices.

arrogant young politician, Poinsett blatantly supported the *yorkinos* whose liberal views were favorable to the United States. To further confirm Mexico´s suspicions, before boundaries had even been legally set, he tried to wrest a territorial agreement from the newly elected Congress, namely – to annex Texas.[25]

In 1824, Spain still refused to recognize Mexico´s independence. The United States and England had rushed to exchange diplomatic relations, sending Ministers and Chargé d´affaires to negotiate favorable trade agreements; France and Germany were fast on their heels. The industrial revolution made for competition among nations whose sights were on expansion of their commerce. Fast steam ships were now crossing the Atlantic. Mexico, so long hermetically sealed off from outside trade, was now ripe to open her doors. The journals of early travelers tell amusing, amazing, frightening and enlightening stories. To hear a language other than Spanish, to see people who were not Spanish, *mestizo* or Indian was a constant source of surprise and curiosity for Mexicans. Very few had traveled abroad and books were a luxury of the rich.

William Bullock, an Englishman writes in 1823:
"The jealousy of the Government of Old Spain so fully succeeded in shutting out Europeans from the knowledge of Mexico that I am acquainted with no book of travels by an Englishman in this country so this journal will, I trust, give a degree of value to my observations. …I sailed from Portsmouth on a mer-

---

25 Poinsette gave name to the Mexican Christmas flower, known in the U.S as "poinsettia".

chant ship chartered by the German Rhenish Company of Merchants, then about to establish themselves in Mexico…. Our first view of the Mexican coast through the telescope was of Veracruz, and towering behind it, a majestic mountain estimated at 17,000 feet. In moments it disappeared in the clouds and we remained like persons just awoke from an extraordinary dream…. The hotel in Veracruz offered wet sheets, no water or lamp so I spent the first night fending off mosquitoes. … I hired a carriage drawn by eight mules for myself, my son, a French gentleman and a servant who spoke French and Spanish…. Drove over almost impassable sections of road…through tropical undergrowth and pinned to the edge of curving mountains….`posadas (inns) offered a thatched roof and a woven mat for a bed surrounded by mules kicking and fighting, barking dogs, fleas and roosters who knew not the time of day,,,,Xalapa and Puebla present a far more beautiful appearance than the cities of Europe…Few women on the streets, all dressed in black, going and coming from the churches with a black veil over their heads….Nothing can surpass the civility of the people…. Mexico City with its magnificent architecture, ornaments reminiscent of Moorish palaces…great mansions with superb chandeliers, carved tables, rugs from the orient, silver goblets …all now passing through the mint in the shape of dollars circulating over Europe and Asia….It is not in the Capital of New Spain that we are to look for the remains of Mexican greatness. Every vestige of its former splendor was annihilated by the conquerors. Cortez was compelled to level to the ground every house as he took *it. and 50.000 Indian workmen followed close to his soldiers to fill the canals with remains. It was the wish of the Spaniards to leave not a trace of former greatness or a recollection of the people they destroyed. It is in the annals of early writers that we know the legends are true….The closing of the mines, the expulsion of the rich Spanish families, the sixteen years of revolutionary warfare, with all the concomitant miseries, have wrought a melancholy alteration in the fortunes of individuals and the general state of the country. But I hope that these times are nearly at an end, and that the period is arriving when Mexico will again exalt her head among the greatest cities of the world, a rank to which she is entitled by her own intrinsic beauty and as the Capital of one of the finest portions of the globe."*

The national economy was in chaos: basic products were scarce, including corn and beans. With the importation of foreign goods, local stores began to be supplied and the small textile and tannery industries revived. The bulk of commerce was the exportation of products such as tobacco, coffee, sugar, vanilla, *cochinilla* (a natural dye long exported by the Spaniards) mahogany and other woods – and above all, silver. The English were quick to negotiate concessions to work the neglected mines, many flooded and abandoned. Money began to flow into the country, ships from many nations were anchoring in Mexican harbors and the mines of Guanajuato, Zacatecas, Pachuca, Taxco and Durango were once more working.. By 1857, 200 mines, sustained by foreign capital and technicians, were producing a significant quantity of silver and gold.

But there was a price to pay: year by year, Mexico´s foreign debt grew. Much capital had fled with the expulsion of the Spaniards. The Constitution had eliminated colonial institutions but not one of the twenty states and four territories in the federation had money to buy or invest. The first loan was negotiated with London bankers at such high interest rates that Mexico only benefited from half the amount of the credit.

In this chaotic period of political upheaval, two institutions, legacies of New Spain, were at the root of bitter debates, blocking the republican experiments. The Church and the Army were both immune from civil law. Until all Mexicans were subject to the same laws, there could be no equality. Since the founding of New Spain, the Church and the Army had enjoyed the privileges known as *fueros*, legal statutes which exempted them from civil jurisdiction; in a word—impunity from the law. In addition, they were exempt from paying taxes.

After Independence in 1821, the Army found itself master of Mexico. But as the economy crumbled, payment to officers was reduced and erratic. The new Federal Army deteriorated into untrained, ill-equipped recruits. It was composed mostly of mestizo and Indian ranks, the majority conscripts supplied by raids on Indian villages. Immune to civil law, they shot civilians and confiscated property as they pleased. Deserters, now bandits, attacked the silver mule trains which trudged from the mines to the Capital while their brother soldiers shot at them. Military tribunals judged offenders according to which side they were on. The Army was the backbone of the barracks uprisings led by caudillos (creole officers), guerilla wars were provoked by caciques (provincial chieftains or political bosses) with their own cadre of soldiers. It was a factional Army whose soldiers were loyal to their leader rather than defenders of the nation. As the century progressed, scores of hungry soldiers deserted. To the three or four million Indians who continued to labor as "peons" on the big haciendas or tried to subsist on their ejido parcels, the word "Independence" was a foreign word.

The Church, no longer subject to clerical appointments made by the Viceroy, assigned its own parish priests, tried matters of the Church in ecclesiastical courts and continued to collect tithes as well as rent from its burgeoning real estate, both incomes exempt from taxes. By mid 1800s nearly half the land in Mexico belonged to the Church.

Those who defended the Church praised its benefits to society. Since times past, priests, monks and nuns had attended a multitude of social services: they built schools and directed education, staffed and administered hospitals, asylums, orphanages, ministered to the Indians and kept family and civil records in parish archives. Weddings, baptisms, funerals, feast days were functions of the Church. José María Luis Mora, an intellectual and outstanding liberal defender of the era, looked upon the Church as a deterrent in the attempt to establish a representative system and build a sense of "nation". He was not against Church doctrine but its practices. "In the parochial schools, a child is encouraged to imitate the lives of the saints. Nothing is taught of patriotism, of civic duties and responsibilities." In diatribes against "a system which is inadequate to form a civic spirit in Mexico", he advocated secular education.

During half a century of factional wars, sincere patriots

rose and fell on the field of political battle, leaving names to be honored by future generations. They were intellectuals and men of integrity who understood their times: Lucas Alamán, José María Luis Mora, Lorenzo Zavala, Fray Servando Teresa de Mier (another priest), Ramos Arizpe and Valentín Gomez Farías are some of the names which stand out on the pages of Mexican history.

Lucas Alamán, a brilliant Conservative, adamantly defended Mexico´s colonial heritage, advocated industrialization but believed in a slow, measured process of transformation. "We have had experience with a monarchy but no experience at all with an elected President." The Liberals were advocating a bureaucracy of governors, secretaries, representatives, local officials and circuit and district judges in a country of seven million inhabitants, five of whom needed no more government than a mayor and a priest. At all cost, radical change should not be allowed! At the other end of the spectrum, the Liberal, Lorenzo de Zavala, with profound faith in the organizational structure of the United States, vociferously advocated shaking off the "vicious" and anachronistic habits of New Spain, particularly privileges of the Church.

Some drastic measures were regretted: in 1827; many *peninsulares* were expelled taking with them their fortunes. In 1829, Spain attempted to reconquer Mexico. Landing in Tampico, the invaders were defeated by General Santa Anna. In a fit of patriotism, all Spaniards were banished from Mexico.

In 1829, when Guadalupe Victoria´s term ended, Vicente Guerrero, Morelos´ other respected General backed by the Federalists, assumed the presidency by insurrection.

After furious infighting, in 1831 control of the Government was seized by a Centralist general. Guerrero was tried and found guilty of heading an illegal government and was executed.

This scenario would be enacted over and over for the next forty-five years. Civil wars, military coups, invasions, uprisings and sheer anarchy would keep Mexico in a state of stagnation. A sense of national identity was an incipient seed.

During this period of cataclysm, one name, above all others, would echo again and again: General Antonio Lopez de Santa Anna. Charismatic, dynamic, fearless, capricious, an inveterate gambler known to keep legislators waiting to attend a cock fight, Santa Anna is one of the most colorful and controversial figures in Mexican history. A creole reared in the royalist ranks, Santa Anna was both the initiator and target of uprisings, hero and traitor. He had supported Iturbide then turned against him, supported the Liberal Republicans then sided with the Conservatives. He changed sides and banners with the fortunes of fate, deserting Congress and retreating to his peaceful hacienda until times again favored his ambitions. It is said that his desire for power was not political ambition but love of acclaim, pageantry and glory. Above all, he loved battle. Always at the head of his troops, he was described by Lucas Alamán as "a good soldier but a bad strategist". As President he was never able to organize a stable government. On a wave of the successful takeover by a powerful group of Liberal reformers, Santa Anna was first elected President in 1833. He was to be in and out of the presidency eleven times from 1833-1855, a key actor in the battles and invasions to come.

TEXAS

While factional conflicts were waged in Congress, a graver problem loomed on the horizon: Texas. That distant northern territory which formed part of the great state of Coahuila had been a constant preoccupation since colonial times. The United States had purchased the enormous Louisiana territory from Napoleon in 1812, doubling its size, and in 1819 acquired Florida from England. Exact borders were undefined. Militant American legislators tried to claim that a portion of Texas was part of the Louisiana purchase while Mexico tenaciously defended her position that Texas was part of her northern territory inherited from Spain long before Louisiana was purchased.

From a practical viewpoint, Mexico knew that her scattered fortress settlements, under constant attack from Indians, offered little resistance should the United States decide to annex Texas. In 1822, the Republic of Mexico granted permission to Moses Austin, an honest, puritan yankee, to bring in Anglo-Saxon settlers in the hope they would become a buffer against the United States. It was the only Mexican territory where slavery was permitted since many of the settlers from the south arrived in Texas with their slaves. The settlers were granted land for allegiance to Mexico. Four conditions prevailed: (1) that they prove they had an honest mode of livelihood (2) that they be Roman Catholics, (3) that they swear obedience to the government of Mexico. (4) That Spanish would be the language of commerce.

Sparsely settled by Spaniards, the territory of Texas was soon overrun by irate Anglo-Saxons whose impatience with Mexico grew over delay in settling land claims and dozens of other complaints. Customs houses and army patrols on the Louisiana border hampered trade so that smuggling and contraband became a way of life. Promising land grants, unscrupulous speculators kept bringing in more settlers. The few priests in the territory, under pressure and threats from the settlers, "converted" settlers as the rule required. "Fer two bucks ya kin let um sprinkle ya and cross ya and yer a Catholic" frontiersman bragged, showing their baptismal certificates. Geographically about 600 miles distant from the Mexican Capital and divided by two extremely different cultures, instead of being a buffer against American expansionism, each day Texas grew closer to the United States. Fighting Comanches and Apaches since their arrival, the Texan frontiersmen were rough, tough and independent minded.

The Texas situation festered. Alarmed by the influx of illegal settlers, Mexico closed the Texas border and levied a higher customs´ tax. Stephen Austin, Moses´ son, offered to try to find a solution to the settlers´ complaints. Loyal to his father´s pledge to Mexico and respected by the settlers, he traveled to the Capital in 1832 to propose a plan that could satisfy both sides: separate Texas from the state of Coahuila, define boundaries and allow it to become an independent state within the Mexican Federation. His petition was ignored. Austin remained in Mexico City determined to obtain an official answer. Finally, as Austin headed back empty handed to Texas, he was arrested and put in jail by Santa Anna who had just taken over the Presidency. Texas would continue to be under the state legislature of Coahuila! When Austin was released in 1835, angry, he returned to Texas where he joined the independence movement. In 1836 the Centralists again took control of the Congress in Mexico City. Texas bolted. Claiming they were Federalists, the Texans declared their independence.

War! It was the only response to such vehement rebellion. But the unstable government had neither the economic resource nor military power in the north to put down the insurrection. Nor was there a strong civilian response to support an army. Provincials took an ambivalent view of politics. Give money or your life to fight for Texas? A thousand kilometers away! Let whoever was in power in the Capital resolve the problem. Congress recognized the immediate need to act. Texas was a key province. At all cost they must protect the northern territories or the United States would slowly infiltrate. They must finance an army. Texas was a tinderbox!

One man responded instantly: General Santa Anna, temporarily out of office, left his hacienda and rapidly raised an army of six thousand as he marched north adding each state´s quota of recruits. As they descended from the highlands and marched through endless stretches of thorny brush and the blazing Coahuila desert, his ill equipped, ill shod and ill fed recruits deserted or died by the hundreds. Santa Anna arrived at the presidio in San Antonio with three thousand men. A motley array of some hundred and fifty armed Texans had congregated in San Antonio, surprised and defeated the garrison and taken possession of an old mission. Santa Anna declared "We will give no quarter to foreigners who have violated all laws and waged war against Mexico." After a siege of thirteen days, the infamous "Battle of the Alamo" was over, every defender slaughtered to the last man, all prisoners killed. Passions ran high. Santa Anna captured the retreating army at Goliad and executed 340 prisoners. Sam Houston quickly gathered the remaining Texas forces and took command as volunteers poured in to the cry of "Remember the Alamo!" The Texans led a final, surprise attack at San Jacinto and ravaged the Mexican army. The defeated Santa Anna was taken prisoner, transported to Washington and made to sign an agreement recognizing Texas´ independence. When it was made known to the President in Mexico, he refused to recognize the agreement, stating that it had not been signed with the sanction of Congress. Mexico refused to recognize Texas´ independence. In disgrace, Santa Anna retired to his hacienda swearing to stay out of politics forever.

The United States was quick to recognize Texas´ secession, an act that created another chasm between the government of the United States and the government of Mexico. Fearing an attempt by Mexico to retake its lost territory, Texas immediately applied for admission to the United States. The request was refused by the Senate which did not wish to admit another slave state to the Union. The controversy over slavery was already a hot issue in the U.S. Congress.

The Texas question was a sharp thorn in the Mexican Congress. Mexico considered Texas a province in revolt. But a country weakened by endless uprisings could not afford to confront a giant. Better to let Texas go, practical politicians reasoned, than give the United States cause to take up arms against Mexico. Tempers flared. The controlling Liberals refused to take heed. They strengthened the patrolling army in "no man´s land", the disputed territory between the Rio Grande and the Nueces River, an area that roughly encompassed half of Texas. The Nueces River had been indicated as the boundary by old Spanish maps. The Mexican Cavalry patrol was ordered to shoot any invaders. They looked for an excuse for a skirmish. Harassment by both sides augmented the tension.

Santa Anna needed to recover his credibility, his admiration. Providentially, France supplied the opportunity. In 1837, the French Minister seized this tense time to pressure Mexico. He demanded 600,000 pesos indemnity suffered by French citizens during the riots of 1828, including 60,000 demanded by a French baker. President Bustamante scoffed at the ludicrous demand claiming it was a pressure play to coerce Mexico into signing a preferential commercial agreement with France. In a week French warships had arrived from the island of Martinique and occupied the port of Veracruz, shelling the old Spanish fortress. Bustamente had no recourse but to declare war. In anger, he said to his secretary, "Why are not the forces of the United States here to break the French blockade? The Monroe doctrine is a farce!"

In his peaceful hacienda, Santa Anna was awakened by a runner crying "War!" *Veracruz* was being bombed by the French! With his usual dynamic reaction, in moments the General was galloping off toward the Gulf port. In the ensuing battle, Santa Anna lost his left leg, amputated beneath the knee. The claim was settled and the ships left; the "Pastry War" won. Disregarding the black banners hung from the balconies of houses warning of cholera on the premises, the citizens of Veracruz rushed into the streets joined by the strident clanging of church bells to acclaim their fallen, beloved hero. A wooden leg was not to deter Santa Anna. He hung another decoration on his uniform and in 1841 assumed the presidency once again.

From 1841 to 1847, endless coups and fierce uprisings saw seven changes of governments and a plethora of interim Presidents in and out of office. A coalition was impossible to achieve. The Centralists, now called Conservatives, were secretly plotting to invite a European Monarch to govern their divided nation. The Federalists, now called Liberals, were adamantly advocating greater liberty for the state legislatures. Strong men with strong convictions made Congress their battleground. Power plays among the generals caused division in the ranks. To exacerbate the problem, Mexico´s foreign loans had soared in addition to indemnities being claimed by the United States, France and England. California was threatening independence while British and French ships roamed her coast waiting to take a foothold. Yucatán was in open revolt. The Mayas, armed by the British in Belice who had their eye on Yucatán, were massacreing whites while the white plantation owners offered to be annexed by the United States in self protection.

For eleven years, the Lone Star Republic of Texas governed itself, ever fighting Indian raids and fearful of Mexico amassing an army to invade and take back their lost territory. In 1845, Texas let it be known that it was considering becoming a protectorate of England. Hastily, the United States offered statehood. The offer was accepted.

Texas was annexed as a slave state, adding the 28th star to the flag of the United States.

On April 7, 1845, a terrible earthquake shook the Capital bringing down the cupola of the Church of Santa Teresa. For three consecutive days violent quakes intermittently continued, creating panic in the city. A portent of disaster the soothsayers prophesied.

CHAPTER X

Probably no page in United States history has been so disputed as the Mexican-American War. "The American Invasion" it is called in Mexican history books. Was it a just war? Or was it a powerful, ambitious neighbor provoking a fight to take advantage of a weak one? Was it the fault of a divided, quarreling nation which had not accepted a reasonable proposal to settle the question of Texas? One thing is indisputable: when it was over in 1848, the map of North America was permanently redrawn: Mexico lost nearly half her territory and the United States became a continental power.

The annexation of Texas created a deeper chasm between Mexico and her powerful northern neighbor. Mexico had never veered from its position that Texas belonged to her northern Spanish territory, hence belonged to Mexico. With annexation, the United States began to look for ways to convince Mexico that Texas´ Independence was an accomplished fact, hence it was now a State of the American Union. The eyes of the world were watching. Was the United States a bully or did it truly embrace democratic principles? The conservative Republicans in the United States´ Congress had held the Texas question at bay hoping for a peaceful solution. In 1846, barely squeezing into office, a tough, sanctimonious, one-minded Democrat became President of the United States. James Polk was convinced that the "Manifest Destiny" of the United States was to sweep westward across the continent expanding the model Republic and giving land to the immigrants that were pouring in. California and the territory between lay in his plans. Frontier forts were quickly built as settlers moved west but the immediate need was to subdue Mexico. He again declared that the land between the Nueces River and the Rio Grande were part of the Louisiana Purchase. The Rio Grande was the only border acceptable to Texas and the United States.

Polk urged settlers to move into the disputed area and sent an army of 3000 men, under the command of General Zachary Taylor, to protect them. Thousands of volunteers, some immigrants just off the boat, joined Taylor who had encamped on the Nueces River near Corpus Christi. Mexican pride and nationalism were inflamed: its Northern Army was instructed to double its forces on the Rio Grande. The waiting game began. If Taylor moved south, Mexico would attack. A skirmish in "no man´s land" in which the Mexican cavalry chased a platoon of Texans and killed several, cocked the trigger. Without really understanding the consequences, war was now inevitable. "American blood has been spilled on American soil" was Polk´s message to

Congress. "We are committed to defend Texas. I ask you to declare war!" Congressman Abraham Lincoln accused Polk of provoking a conflict at the Rio Grande. He decried the warlike fever that embraced American society. Mexican President Herrera tried to convince his colleagues to accept the loss of Texas. "War with the United States is a bottomless abyss into which all hopes for the future will disappear", he argued. To no avail, national pride was at stake.

Engaging pockets of Mexican resistance, Taylor marched his army south to Matamoros on the Gulf of Mexico. Seasoned by years of fighting Indian wars, Zachary Taylor was a tough, fearless, astute leader, in command of a cadre of trained soldiers who had the best artillery and weapons available. The weak northern Mexican army could put up little resistance. The Americans built a fort, known as Fort Brown, to defend their position.[26] Moving south, Taylor stormed Monterrey in a furious battle which took civilian lives and left deep scars in the hearts of its inhabitants. Monterrey surrendered. Taylor moved further south, and after taking Saltillo, encamped in an open space near the town to await orders. Polk ordered Taylor to cede half his army to General Winfield Scott who would sail down to Veracruz; disembark and follow the road up through the mountains to Mexico City. The Gulf would be secured by a naval blockade of Mexican ports. Mexico had no ships that could challenge them. Always on the alert, with half his men gone, Taylor awaited further orders.

Informed of Taylor´s position, Santa Anna removed his sash of office and donned his uniform. Now 52 with

---

26 Fort Brown became the city of Brownsville, Texas, across the border from Matamoros.

a wooden leg in the stirrup, he headed north, gathering 20,000 men through state quotas. Outnumbering Taylor´s army three to one, Santa Anna approached Saltillo.

> *An eagle began to descend, circling, circling where a young Mexican conscript sat resting. "Look, an eagle!" he cried out to his companion, a smile lighting his sweat-streaked face. "It´s a good omen," he declared. "Not that one," his companion replied. "It´s not one of ours. It´s a northern eagle diverted south." The bugle sounded to continue the march. With resignation, they slung their rifles over their shoulders. They had not eaten in two days and their water canteens were empty.*

Taking his enemy by surprise, Santa Anna attacked. It was a long, intense battle. Santa Anna rode up and down the lines brandishing his sword, encouraging his raw troops. The battle was a stalemate, neither side letting up. By nightfall both exhausted armies encamped. Without shutting an eye, Taylor awaited the dawn, wondering if he would survive the day. But dawn revealed only Santa Anna´s fires smoldering. He had retreated. Like Hidalgo on the road to Mexico City, Santa Anna´s decision to return to the Capital is incomprehensible to military analysts. Many claim he could have defeated Taylor right then and there. His own explanation was that his men could not endure another day of battle. But more important, he claimed he was recalled to defend the Capital and restore law and order. Congress had approved the seizure and sale of Church properties to fund the war bringing the wrath of the Conservatives down on their heads! And General Scott was coming up from Veracruz.

A hurricane in Veracruz destroyed the triumphal arch which had been raised to Santa Anna´s victory over the French and his statue lay shattered on the cobblestones when Winfield Scott and his troops landed. Circling the old walled city with cannon emplacements, a devastating bombardment quieted the old Spanish fort and the city surrendered. The young cadets of the Naval Academy fought courageously but the Americans outgunned them. Many fell defending their city. More American soldiers were lost to yellow fever than to the Mexican defense.

Now Scott headed for the mountains along the route that Cortés had followed. Parrots, macaws and the exotic aroma of the tropics lay below them as soldiers hauled their cumbersome artillery over precipices, canyons and dizzying heights.

Santa Anna was ready. He waited for them on the outskirts of the city of Puebla. For once he had sufficient arms, food and money to pay his soldiers. He knew the terrain; his fortified position was impenetrable. Seasoned, capable officers warned him that he had left his rear flank exposed. But he ignored their advice; it faced the woods, on the edge of a ravine. What Santa Anna had overlooked was the flexibility of the modern American artillery. After days of scouting the area, two of Scott´s engineers, Colonel Robert E. Lee and Lieutenant P. T. Beauregard, advised the General that it was feasible to clear a road and position the guns in what appeared to be impassable terrain. Santa Anna was attacked in the rear flank and soon surrounded. The Mexicans were cut to ribbons, forced to retreat and disperse, leaving behind all of their weaponry, even the clean uniforms they had acquired. Streams of prisoners were escorted to Veracruz. Scott sent a messenger to Polk saying, "The Mexicans no longer have an army". Humbled and defeated, Santa Anna escaped and made his way to Mexico City.

Scott marched on to Puebla, citadel of the Catholic Church. After quick deliberation and pressure from the Bishop, the Governor of Puebla asked for a vote: "Either we fight to the death, leaving rivers of blood in our streets, our Cathedral in ruins, or we surrender and save our lives and our city. If the Americans are defeated, we will raise our flag again". Rather than expose their beautiful city to shelling and the slaughter of civilians, Puebla surrendered to the American troops.

In Washington, Congress debated the justice and purpose of the war. Congressmen Abraham Lincoln and Daniel Webster called it an act of aggression. Senator Henry Clay declared it "a war of offensive aggression. Mexico is defending its firesides, castles and altars."

Simultaneously, with Taylor´s march southeast down the Gulf coast of Mexico, the Western Army of the United States had set out with long pack trains, horses, mules, wagons and artillery on a 1400 mile trek along the Santa Fe Trail from Chihuahua to California. The Santa Fe trail and the old Spanish "Camino Real" were both valuable trade routes. Already the flag of the United States was being planted along the way. Telegraph wires buzzed with uprisings in California. Lincoln called the march "a precipitated maneuver through Mexican territory". "An immediate and honorable peace must be sought," he advocated. A resolution was finally passed to offer to buy certain territories and halt the war. Pay for peace. Polk sent a representative to offer 30 million dollars for California, New Mexico and Texas to the Rio Grande. Outraged when they learned of the proposal, the Mexican Government refused to receive the representative and sent him packing back to Washington. Polk was now convinced that the Mexicans would never stop fighting until the Capital was taken.

In Puebla, Scott looked down from Cortes´ Pass at the foot of the snow-covered volcanoes. Like a painting in the transparent atmosphere, he could see the Valley of Mexico - extensions of cornfields and agaves, white, fortress-like haciendas dispersed through the land . The Capital lay in the distance close to three glimmering lakes.

Scott threatened his troops with severe punishment for misconduct. They were quartered. They rested. The people of Puebla did not complain. American soldiers were dazzled by the richness and opulence of the churches. "But most to be admired," one soldier wrote, "is the equality of all ranks before the altar. Mexicans seem more loyal to their Church than to their country." The clergy viewed the American Protestants as "invaders who have no moral principals or religious creed." Catholics among the soldiers felt great sympathy for the Mexicans.

For three months, Scott waited for supplies, fresh horses and reinforcements. Few arrived as guerrillas ambushed patrols along the road to Veracruz. With a reinforced army, General Taylor was now marching toward Mexico City.

Cut off from supplies, with an army of only 10,000, Scott made a difficult decision: he began his descent into the Valley of Mexico.

Although Santa Anna could not win battles he could raise armies. Swallowing his shame he determined to contain Scott. First, he must meet and defeat Taylor on the outskirts of Mexico City. Quickly, Santa Anna raised an army of 18,000 men. The encounter with Taylor was a series of ravaging battles with enormous losses on both sides. Although superior in number but against superior artillery and guns, the bloody battles of Churubusco, Molino del Rey and Chapultepec finally decimated the Mexican forces. American casualties were heavy. A battalion of Irish-Americans known as the "St. Patrick Battalion" defected to the Mexican side as did other American Catholics, morally unable to kill fellow Catholics. Those caught were hanged as deserters. Some young Mexican military cadets leaped to their death from the parapets of Chapultepec Castle rather than be taken prisoners, thus creating future heroes known as "Los Niños Héroes" (The Boy Heroes). Today an impressive monument can be seen at the foot of the Castle in Chapultepec Park.

The remnants of the Battle of Chapultepec now regrouped to face Scott, not three miles away. Adding to their ranks were patriotic creole and mestizo volunteers, artisans and laborers willing to wage their lives in defense of their country. Political differences were buried. Rapidly built barricades were raised. 4000 men reported to headquarters as Santa Anna assumed command with the patriotic determination of a true national leader.

"Do you hear the bugles and drums, papá? It´s the signal that all men between 15 and 60 should report now to form brigades. You and I and grandfather will

defend the city together!" young Ramón shouted picking up a rifle he had never fired. Martial music blasted as civilian ranks marched out to key positions. The populace shouted "Vivas!" running alongside them on the streets and tearful mothers shouted "Go with God!" as they waved to their men from balconies and doorways. They fought valiantly, desperately, but one position after another fell as the Americans battled their way through, entering the city. The church bells, silent for days, now tolled a warning of the approaching invading forces. In the distance a military band was playing "Green Grow the Grasses Oh!" The "gringos" were coming! Closer now, "Yankee Doodle Dandy" was sung by an endless stream of soldiers as they battled through the streets and marched toward the zócalo and the Palace. Ragged children dug up cobblestones to throw at the foreigners, frightened citizens locked themselves in and the more audacious ran to the rooftops to hurl rocks and insults down on the straggly looking "gringos". A water-carrier, with a bucket hanging from each end of a long pole balanced across his shoulders, dumped his water on passing soldiers in the only act of harassment he could muster. Collective anger brought people together. "Now I know how the Aztecs must have felt," someone remarked…. By nightfall, the exhausted defenders and invaders stopped fighting.

Weary but unscathed, Ramón, his father and grandfather returned to the house. Grief and pain were mirrored in their eyes. "I was with Morelos at the battle of Cuautla," the old man said. "I watched the Archbishop place the Crown of Independence on Iturbide's head.

I was in Congress when our 1824 Constitution was drafted - how long ago, 22 years? Now our nation may cease to be." Tears obscured his eyes. "Will Mexico only be remembered as a meteor that flashed through the sky and disappeared in the United States?"

On the morning of September 16, Independence Day, the flag of the United States flew over the Palace. A strange silence came over the city. Perhaps inured to war, perhaps with resignation, the citizens waited. Their city was under siege. The Church looked on with indifference; General Scott had declared he would not interfere in matters of religion. There were those on both sides of the border who hoped the stars and stripes would remain: U.S. zealots wanted the whole country to be annexed and numerous disillusioned Mexicans whispered that Mexico might be better off as a protectorate of the United States. Patriots urged Congress to agree on terms and sign a peace treaty. Expel the Americans! Guerrillas were still attacking and it could go on forever.

In February, 1848, the Treaty of Guadalupe Hidalgo was signed and ratified by the Congress. Mexico ceded half her territory: Upper California, New Mexico and Texas to the Rio Grande. In return, the United States paid Mexico fifteen million dollars and cancelled the indemnity demands.

The nation had survived. Mexicans filled the churches to give thanks to God. The Mexican flag flew over the Palace as well as in her ports and towns. Now they must build a new nation. They must pull together.

For five years there was a singular absence of rebellions as Santa Anna retired and, in a peaceful change of government, an honest moderate took charge of the Liberal government. To forestall another attempt to retake the Presidency, Santa Anna was exiled to Venezuela. He took with him his medals and his fighting cocks. The Liberals were in solid control.

Suddenly, Easter week of 1852, a raging fire broke out near the center of the city, destroying four square city blocks. In June, cholera struck with a vengeance, killing nearly 7000 citizens in three months.... Was this God's wrath for ousting the Conservatives, the defenders of the Church? Pox on the heads of the Liberals who had seized and sold Church properties!

Resentment and differences were deeply rooted in two incompatible political views. The Conservatives wanted to pour new ideas into old molds. The Liberals wanted to break the old molds. Secretly, the Spanish Minister negotiated a loan for the new brand of Conservatives, the Monarchists. The Minister urged them to take over and bring a member of the Spanish Royal family to rule as an independent monarch. Brazil had proved it could be done. Wisely, Lucas Alamán, the scholarly, experienced pillar of the Conservatives, realized that such a move would plunge the country into anarchy. For now, a stable government was imperative. The United States was busy laying railroad track and pushing west. Foreign investment was converting it into a rich nation. In Mexico, only the mines, sugar and textile mills were sustaining a feeble economy. The British bondholders must be dealt with, roads built, new machinery purchased. Bitterly, Lucas Alamán stated "We are a nation that has gone from infancy to decrepitude in 30 years". The moderate government was doing its best, but a strong hand at the helm was needed. In 1853 the Liberals´ term was ending and flaming tempers were again about to explode. After long deliberation, Alamán concluded that the only political figure who could hold the country together was - Antonio Lopez de Santa Anna. Overwhelmingly outnumbered in Congress, the Liberals were forced to agree. Surely after thirty years of war and now 58 years old, he would act with patriotism and reason. Alamán forced the approval of an unprecedented one year period for Santa Anna to act as absolute dictator. Enough time to find a monarch. Santa Anna was recalled from exile.

Handsome, proud, charismatic, Santa Anna entered the Capital in his resplendent carriage by the road that led from the Shrine of Guadalupe. Fireworks burst in the air, choirs of children sang and from balconies and carriages, beautiful young ladies threw flowers as he passed. He took over the Presidency with all the pomp and ceremony of a King, bestowing upon himself the title of "His Serene Highness". To celebrate his return to office a new National Theater was built and the Italian opera season was brilliant. As testimony to his patriotism, Santa Anna convoked a contest for a national anthem. The words were written by a Mexican and the music by a Spaniard. It was sung for the first time in Santa Ana´s National Theater. Ignoring his wife, beautiful young women fawned over him, orators wrote and declaimed poems to his exalted person while the wealthy creole class honored him with gifts and flatteries in return for favors. He was assaulted by those who wished to take control of his agenda.

In June of 1853, Lucas Alamán suddenly died. Now

there was no one to restrain His Serene Highness. Transferring money from public works, he increased the army to 90.000 and brought over Spanish and Prussian officers to train it. His Palace guard wore the uniforms of the Vatican´s Swiss guards, his carriages were magnificent. With his extravagant lifestyle of an Imperial Court, the coffers of the nation were rapidly depleted. Again, Santa Anna was saved. The United States offered to buy the southern strip of Arizona through which they wished to extend the railroad line. The United States now stretched from coast to coast and needed to connect the continent. Santa Anna signed the "Gadsen Treaty" in 1853. Ten million dollars entered the national coffers.[27]

His year was coming to an end. Santa Anna tried to extend his dictatorship one more year. There were those who wanted to crown him the second Emperor, Antonio I. But an opposition storm was brewing, gathering force. He sensed its strength; it came from an uncompromising conviction - control of Congress and a new Constitution was the objective. Twice, Santa Ana marched out to crush the rebels and twice returned. Searching for the enemy was like smoke, asphyxiating. They hid, they scattered to another place. They were everywhere.

Gaslights, the latest in illumination, lit the foyer of the National Theater. In magnificent dress uniforms, lancers lined the stairs and elegant ladies bowed as their Serene Highnesses ascended and occupied their

---

27 The United States was putting pressure on Santa Anna to sell a larger part of territory, but he only accepted to sell "La Mesilla" to be used for the construction of American railways.

gilded baroque box. Other boxes were occupied by Santa Anna's special entourage of aristocrats and wealthy businessmen to whom he had conceded the sugar and tobacco monopolies, customs collections and other lucrative enterprises that assured their support. Before the play ended, a courier opened the door and whispered in the President's ear: "There has been an uprising in Guerrero, a pronouncement against you backed by Ignacio Comonfort. He is marching toward the Capital."

Santa Anna slipped out of the theater, changed into ordinary clothes, caged his fighting cocks, packed his medals and headed for Veracruz and a ship. Intuitively he realized that this was a different rebellion, a revolution that would not include him. The South Americans considered him a hero, the Napoleon of the West. They would shield him.

He lived too long. After eighteen years of exile, moving from Colombia to the Caribbean, every attempt to return to Mexico repelled, Santa Anna was finally allowed to live his last days on his beloved hacienda. Forgotten, penniless, his loyal wife paid old soldiers to come with words of adulation and recall his glory. Santa Anna died in 1876 at the age of 82. In his memoirs he wrote: "Man is nothing. Power is everything."

CHAPTER XI

Mysterious influences have always marked Mexico´s history: the great Mayan Empire disappeared, the teotihua-canos, builders of majestic pyramids, vanished, the Toltecs fell when Quetzalcoatl was driven out. It was the belief that Cortés could be his reincarnation that contributed to the fall of the Aztec Empire and birth of New Spain.

By mid-nineteenth century, New Spain was only a shadow. From the time of Independence, 1821, the new Republic had vacillated between the Conservatives and the Liberals leaving fissures and divisions in an ever-changing government without the power to make necessary and permanent changes. By 1855, the arbitrary and despotic acts of Santa Anna in his last term in office, led to another revolt, this time the clash of irreconcilable ideals.

In the darkness and gloom of chaos, the light of a clear dawn was glowing over the mountains of Oaxaca where two native sons had grown to manhood. Benito Juárez, a

Zapotec Indian, and Porfirio Díaz, a mestizo of humble origen, were to take center stage in the drama that unfolded in the last half of the XIX century.

A new generation, which had no personal memory of colonial days, was taking over. Young mestizos were replacing the old creoles. They were lawyers, engineers, scientists, doctors, educated in excellent secular institutions neither ingrained in Indian culture nor loyal to Spanish ideals. Fiercely patriotic, they were convinced that installation of a permanent Federal Government would bring the long desired order, stability and progress to their country. Reform was in order. The Church and the Army must be brought under civil authority. The Church owned more than half the territory of Mexico! .A Federal Army, loyal to a government based on well-defined, democratic principles, would put an end to anarchy and save Mexico from gradual annexation by the United States. Reform was the mood. Reform was imperative!

Oaxaca is a land unto itself, a southern State spread high in the mountains, extending in the west to the Pacific Ocean and in the east to the State of Veracruz on the Gulf of Mexico. Twenty native languages were spoken, as different from each other as German from Chinese. Its Capital, built by Spaniards, lies in a temperate valley and is a citadel of baroque architecture. Its´ magnificent baroque church and convent of Santo Domingo was recently totally restored. Of the ethnic cultures which were dominant, the Zapoteca was the strongest, long ago having subjugated the warrior tribe of Mixtecas. The Zapotecas were ancient politicians and merchants who have survived to this day as an intelligent, strong people. It was a Zapotec Indian who was to change the course of Mexico.

Benito Juárez was born in 1806. It is said he was descended from noble Zapotec lineage. His parents died when he was three. An uncle permitted him to become his goat herder and live under his roof. At the age of fourteen, Benito left his environment where spiny cactus abounded and made his way to Oaxaca City where his sister was a servant in the house of a wealthy Spaniard who welcomed him and gave him work. Recognizing his quick mind and desire to learn, a book-binder took Benito under his wing and sent him to school. He quickly learned to read and write in Spanish. Top of his class, the only further education open to him was Seminary where Indians could aspire to be priests. The doctrine taught in New Spain had changed little: blind obedience to the Church and the Central Authority. The Church had gobbled up the ancestral lands of the Indians and bad governments had reduced his people to ignorance and poverty. Benito left the study of Latin and theology and signed up as a law student in the new lay University of Arts and Sciences.

Sitting in the central plaza, listening to the military band, Benito noticed men he admired, men people whispered were mysterious Masons, regularly meeting in a great house on the square. He struck up conversations and was invited to join them. He was a devout Catholic but in his view religion should be a private matter, the Church had no right to dictate every comma and period. As a Mason, this individualistic view was strengthened.

Benito Juárez was admired by his fellow citizens. He was honest, prudent, solemn, fair. He was elected to the local State Legislature, going straight up the ladder to become Governor of Oaxaca. At age thirty-seven he married a daughter of the Spaniard who had befriended him. An Indian had courted and married a creole! Severe, with heavy chiseled features, Juárez has been compared to a stone idol. Convinced that the law must apply to all equally, his style of governing was ethical and fair. Firm in his convictions, he was incorruptible.

Claiming "States´Rights", Benito Juárez denied Santa Anna the right to march his army through Oaxaca in his frantic search to flush out the young Liberals gathered along the Pacific near Acapulco. Exercising his absolute authority as Dictator of the nation, Santa Anna had Juárez arrested and sent into exile. Juárez made his circuitous way, via Mexico City and Veracruz, to New Orleans where he remained for nearly a year. It is said he worked in a cigar factory to feed himself. His letters to his wife reveal his deep suffering in this "state of limbo". He had no money to send home. His family lived out their exile with friends in New York. With scarcely enough to feed them, two sons died during this period.

Fate placed in Benito Juárez´ path another exiled Governor, Melchor Ocampo of Michoacán., a world-traveled scholar and scientist with a passion for social justice. Ocampo became Juárez´ lifelong friend and supporter. After Santa Anna fled into exile and the militant Reformers took over the Government, Juárez and Ocampo returned to Mexico and were named to Cabinet positions by the provisional President of the new Liberal party, General Ignacio Comonfort.

It was General Comonfort who had led the coup

d´état. He was a wealthy creole educated by the Jesuits, a well-liked, conciliatory man. His task was to form a Constitutionalist Congress which would write a new Constitution for Mexico. They came from all over the country, representatives and their substitutes from 29 states and territories, Moderate and Radical Liberals joined by a few Moderate Conservatives. Mostly middle class, they were lawyers, doctors, newspapermen, merchants, the majority inclined to favor a measured political transition. A few old rabid Liberals, like Gomez Farías, Guillermo Prieto and poet Ignacio Ramirez lent brilliant oratory to the debates. It was Comonfort´s task to meld this group into a working Constitutionalist Congress. To crush the Monarchists was urgent.

The Church was number one on the agenda. Comonfort assigned a capable economist, Lerdo de Tejada, to write a new law which would legalize land reform. The law was quickly ratified by Congress. La Ley Lerdo in essence "took back" Church property as well as large tracks of land belonging to foreign corporations. These properties would be put up for sale at an assessed price. Once sold, the previous owner would receive the assessed price and pay a heavy property tax to the Government. It was devised to create a strong middle class of property owners and provide revenue for the government. Confiscation with compensation, a fair transaction made into law.

La Ley Lerdo caused an explosion! On its heels, La Ley Juárez placed the Church and the Army under civil law. The Church burst with anger! It would accept nothing.! No dialogue! No conciliatory meetings! Excommunication for all who approved the laws or bought Church property! The

Constitutionalists were labeled "Anti-Christ" and diatribes against them raged from every pulpit.

The Congress continued to meet. The question of religious freedom arose, there were many foreign immigrants living and working in Mexico. "To open our doors to other religions would shake the very foundation of our society!" Comonfort argued. The article was not adopted. All agreed that the President should be elected for four years, not to run twice in succession and to be succeeded, when necessary, by the President of the Supreme Court. Unanimously, the first article of the new Constitution was drafted and ratified:

"THE MEXICAN NATION RECOGNIZES THAT THE RIGHTS OF MAN ARE THE BASIS AND OBJECTS OF SOCIAL INSTITUTIONS. AS SUCH, IT DECLARES THAT ALL LAWS AND ALL AUTHORITIES OF THE NATION MUST RESPECT AND SUSTAIN THE GUAR-ANTEES GRANTED BY THIS CONSTITU-TION."

The Church was the touchy problem: heated discussions flared every day.

"Religion is the glue that holds Mexico together! The Church civilized this country, why be so hard on it?" the moderates debated. "The role of the Church is spiritual guidance not economic dominance!" the radicals replied. "And who has money to buy Church properties?" the moderates continued. "The rich won´t risk excommunication". Constituents worked avidly to define the new laws: the

rights of the individual, freedom of the press, free education, the right to vote…."Education is the root. We have
95 percent illiteracy. How can an illiterate majority vote?
Politicians will buy their votes. Education must be first….
Gentlemen, the mission of this Congress today is to bring
the Church and the Military under the jurisdiction of civil
authority in all cases that apply. No more impunity!"

A rowdy gallery listened and shouted either insults or
approval. It was difficult to maintain a quorum. Joining
the outcries of the Church, the old Conservatives waved
their banner: Family, Church and State! Protect our sacred institutions! In their eyes, the Liberals seemed to be
promulgating a promiscuous society where "equal rights"
meant each individual could do as he pleased and "freedom
of worship" meant letting the Protestants in and God knew
who else to follow! Priests began to hide arms in the store-
rooms of monasteries and rile the populace to use them
against the Anti-Christs. Monasteries and convents were
seized and the dazed monks and nuns shipped off to Spain.
Wives wept and pleaded with their husbands not to sign.[28]

*A dim oil lamp made a futile attempt to illuminate
the altar in the small chapel. In front of the altar a few
flames flickered in votive glasses, the wax long melted. It
was dark in the pew where the wife of a young peasant
soldier prayed. Her husband had volunteered to join the
Conservative Army to defend the Church. She wrung
her hands in despair. "Holy father protect him," she*

---

28 The Holy See allowed the people to swear to the Constitution in
order not to lose their jobs, but only asked them not to accept it their heart
and conscience.

prayed. "He is fighting for you.

In the Cathedral of Mexico City a well-dressed woman knelt and prayed. Her husband was a young Liberal delegate who was being pressed to sign the Constitution. "Oh sweet Mother of God, don´t let him sign it! How could we live without the assurance of a Christian burial, the priest´s blessing in marriage, in baptism. We would be denied communion, last rites, our children would be forbidden to attend the parochial school. What would life be!"

While the Constitutionalists debated, the Monarchists were in Europe seeking a Catholic Prince to rule them, and in the countryside of Mexico poor and rich were being armed by the Church. On February 5, 1857, the new Constitution was finally ratified and sworn to in front of a crucifix. Old Gomez Farías attended in a wheel chair. Reform had won. Comonfort was elected President and Benito Juárez President of the Supreme Court. The next day the Conservatives declared the Constitution invalid. From Rome, Pope Pius IX attacked the new Constitution. Conservative representatives in Europe increased their search for an Emperor, any Emperor, who, with no partisan interests, could bring peace to their divided land. In Mexico, the Conservative uprising could no longer be ignored. Comonfort, who had hoped to reconcile both sides and failed, resigned as President and left in self-exile.

Comonfort left Mexico as the Conservative Generals were amassing their troops. Juárez barely had time to move from his seat in the Supreme Court to the Presidential chair when they were already in the Palace. All the members of the Congress were herded into the halls and arrested. Juárez escaped by seconds. His black carriage was seen racing along the road to Querétaro, the enemy in close pursuit. In Querétaro he was given a hero´s welcome and proclaimed by the local Legislature to be the legitimate President of the Republic. He continued on to Guadalajara where he was nearly executed by fanatic Catholics, on to the Pacific port of Manzanillo, packet boat to Panama, across the Isthmus, across to Havana on a passenger ship, across again to New Orleans and down to Veracruz on another passenger ship. There he established his government, soon to be joined by a quorum of congressmen. Determined, at cost of his life, Benito Juárez pledged to uphold and govern by the new Constitution. The law was above all else. To deprive his enemies of the most lucrative revenue in Mexico, he took over the customs´ houses and blocked their delivery of arms. While civil war raged all around him, Juárez decided to conclude the Reform. Henceforth all properties of the Church – land, convents, monasteries, hospitals, schools, haciendas and all commercial enterprises belonged to the nation. Freedom of religion was guaranteed. Civil registry of birth, marriage and death became compulsory.[29] The Liberal Congress ratified the new laws. With money from the customs houses, Juárez bought arms for his troops whose ranks swelled every day. Most of the country was with the Liberals. In Veracruz Juárez ruled "under the law" and in Mexico City the Conservatives ruled with God on their side. Two governments, two opposing political convictions.

29 Today in Mexico, most couples marry twice: once in a civil ceremony, and the second, with all the trimmings, by the Church which only has the right to bless the union performed by the State. The Church does not own even the property on which their parochial churches are built.

What started out as a peaceful reform ended with a vengeance against the Church and the Conservatives. The "War of the Reform" was the longest and bloodiest war in the forty years of constant battles since Independence. For three years it raged. It divided the country. Destroyed altars and decapitated saints were relics of this bitterly fought war. It was a civil war that would determine the road Mexico was to follow.

As night fell, an old man trudged through burnt fields and walked up the tree-lined path to his house. He crossed the patio, threw back a heavily bolted door and entered his world - walls covered with fine damask and exquisite paintings. A large gilded mirror reflected the flicker of candles in a crystal chandelier proving that at least one of his servants was still alive.. In an alcove at the far end of the room hung a magnificent crucifix. He walked toward the gold leaf altar and knelt at the Pri Dieux. "They are coming. Give me courage, God,"he prayed. " Let me die like a Christian soldier." Across the burnt field where his peons lived, a young Indian woman ran into a burning hut to rescue her baby. Her husband staggered through the ruins to find the charred body of his family.

The Conservatives had well-trained Generals, more experienced troops, better discipline, more money. The Church supplied money and rallied the Indians to their cause. Village against village, ranchers against guerrillas, the provinces against the cities. Unbridled destruction and plunder. The Conservatives soon took the major cities of the central plateau and scattered territories in the south and north. They declared victory only to face the Liberals in another city. Always in need of funds and ammunition, the Liberal troops hung in. Twice with the enemy at his door in Veracruz, Juárez , too, hung in. The United States recognized his Republican Government as the legitimate Government of Mexico and sent Juárez arms.

On December 22, 1860, the last battle was fought. Both sides, exhausted and depleted of men and money, met near Mexico City. With unprecedented valor and luck, the Liberals won. The Conservatives surrendered. Juárez packed up and without fanfare returned to the Capital in his black carriage. On Christmas day he reinstalled the Liberal Federal government in the Palace.

Juárez´ dream of peace and prosperity quickly blew away with the wind. The only inheritance of his triumphant government was economic bankruptcy. Mines were abandoned, crops going to rot, industry and commerce at a standstill. His principal Generals were being kidnapped and executed including Melchor Ocampo, his staunch friend who had returned to his hacienda only to be killed by vengeful guerrillas. The State Legislatures offered only debts. Money from the properties seized from the Church, instead of being used for roads and schools, had been wasted on war. The country was in ruins, the internal debt had soared and the external debt was monumental! Half the Congress asked for Juárez´ resignation but he hung in. Nine months after he returned to office, Juárez was forced to take an unprecedented measure: he declared a moratorium on payment of the foreign debt. He advised the Ministers of France, England and Spain of his decision causing an uproar in the European community.

France, England and Spain had new grievances against both the Liberals and the Conservatives. Spanish hacendados had been killed and their lands taken, adding to Spain´s resentments against its former colony. A Conservative General had seized an English silver train and later robbed the English Legation. French investors had made loans to the Conservatives, including Napoleon III´s half brother, and Juárez refused to recognize the Conservatives´ debts. Mexico needed a lesson! Meeting in London, the three European nations decided to take over the customs houses in Veracruz and Tampico until Mexico agreed to all debts and immediate payment.

The first ships arrived in December, 1862. Troops disembarked and were encamped. Aware of his fragile state, Juárez sent a desperate message to his friend, President Abraham Lincoln, to invoke the Monroe Doctrine and drive out the Europeans. Lincoln´s reply to his friend and neighbor was short: "I need every ship to protect our own harbors." The American Civil War had started. Juárez decided to take a conciliatory position with his European "guests" and offered to renegotiate the debt. England and Spain signed the final draft and sailed out of Veracruz. The French had other plans. With permission they had encamped a large force up in the hills to escape the yellow fever. Juárez expected them to sail with the French delegation soon.

Aware of the constant anarchy Mexico had endured and the sincere desire of reputable Mexicans to bring order and lasting peace to their country, Napoleon III and his counselors convinced themselves that an invasion of

Mexico was justified. The Mexican delegation had assured him that he could overthrow the Liberals in a matter of months. On the practical side there would be welcome economic recompense. Mexico´s silver had maintained the Spanish throne for three hundred years. French investors would flock to the new American Empire. Morally, they would bring stability to a country in constant revolution. A Catholic Monarch would fortify the Latin culture and prevent the Anglo-Saxons from taking over. The Liberals were thieves plundering a Catholic nation! Now would be a perfect time to invade without interference from the United States which was bogged down in its own Civil War. The Mexican nation would be happy, the Church would be happy and his investors would be happy. His Mexican venture could well be "the most beautiful page" in his reign. He had a Prince in mind., one who would surely accept. Without further hesitation, Napoleon III embarked six thousand troops to back up the contingent already stationed in Veracruz.

In little more than a year, the triumphant Constitutionalists had a bankrupt, divided, disoriented government about to face the might of the most powerful army in the world.

CHAPTER XII

Gazing out at the Adriatic sea from his palace, Miramar, Prince Ferdinand Maximilian Hapsburg put away the catalogue of botanical specimens he had been working on and watched the billowing sails of a small ship head for Trieste. His gaze was distant – focused on a country far across the Atlantic ocean: Mexico. A delegation from that country had just left. The offer they made him was tempting. If only he had been born the first son instead of the second, today he would be King of the mighty Austro-Hungarian Empire. But life had not been dull: as Commander of the Imperial Navy, he had traveled widely, called on his cousin Victoria, Queen of England, visited numerous other royal relatives in Europe and crossed the Mediterranean to North Africa. Later, he crossed the Atlantic to call on his cousin the Emperor of Brazil. He had been fascinated with South America and felt great empathy for the poor living in those countries. What an enormous responsibility governing there must entail! What would he face? Since its Independence in 1821, Mexico had lived in a state of constant upheaval to the extent that it had lost half its territory. He had been assured that as Emperor he would be received with fiestas and flowers; the entire nation was ready to welcome a monarch who would bring peace and stability. His beautiful young wife, Carlota, daughter of the King of Belgian, was an ambitious young lady, ready to take her place as Empress of Mexico. She had encouraged him to accept. Napoleon had assured him that the remaining Liberal rebels would soon be put down and Mexico pacified, prepared to receive him. The French army was already fighting in Mexico.

The campesinos gawked as they watched the disciplined French soldiers in red caps march up the mountain toward Mexico City, the same mountains that had been climbed by Cortés and General Scott. As they marched higher, anger began to take hold and guerrillas began to harass the French Army. Waiting in the city of Puebla, General Ignacio Zaragoza had quartered his ragtag army. Leading a large army of volunteers, the seasoned Liberal warrior from Oaxaca, Porfirio Díaz, offered Zaragoza his support. They fortified the city and waited. On May 5, overconfident, the French General launched his troops in a frontal attack at the center of the Mexican fortifications only to be cut down on all sides and forced to retreat – all the way back to Veracruz. One thousand bodies, wearing crosses and medals from Magenta, Austerlitz and Crimea, were testimony to the determination of the Mexicans to resist. A miracle had happened – the Mexicans had defeated the most powerful army in the world! That victory at Puebla added an important holiday to the Mexican calendar, May 5, 1862.

But jubilation was short lived. Napoleon was committed and sent thirty thousand troops under the command of one of his ablest generals, General Forey. Seven months later, Forey took the city of Puebla and marched on to Mexico City. .

Benito Juárez looked out the window of his office in the Palace. Across the zócalo, in the distance, he could hear drums and bugles. For a second his eyes flinched. He could surrender or escape. His stone face froze into a determined expression. Hastily he left instructions for his Ministers and Army, gathered up the Constitution, the archives and what was left in the treasury, got into his black carriage and left by the back entrance. He would not surrender! He would establish his government elsewhere. He had done it before. Zaragoza was dead but Porfirio Díaz had escaped and would hold Oaxaca and the south. Again the familiar black carriage was seen on the road, followed by loyal members of his cabinet. Juárez headed north.

General Forey and his resplendent, triumphant army were welcomed like heroes by the citizens of the Capital. Weary of years of turmoil, they looked upon Forey as a savior. The bells of the Cathedral rang joyously and smoke from incense rose in the churches as prayers were offered for the victors. A Regency of Notables was quickly named to rule until the arrival of an Emperor, a matter still not settled.

Maximilian deliberated: should he accept, his brother, Franz Joseph, had asked him to resign his right of succession to the Austrian throne. Many had warned him that Mexico was a fickle, perennially bankrupt and ungovernable country. They warned that once the Civil War was over, the United States would not tolerate an Empire across its border. He needed the assurance of military support… Carlota was bored and eager to start a new life: she was advancing rapidly in her studies of Spanish and Mexican history. She assured him that he had a dynastic right to the throne of Mexico. King Charles V was a Hapsburg and look what glory he had brought to Spain and Mexico… But his would be a liberal Empire, Maximilian fantasized, where justice and order would prevail. He would make Mexico into a modern, educated nation and bring renewed respect and glory to the Hapsburg family.

In 1862 Maximilian advised the Mexican delegation that he accepted the offer – with certain conditions: he asked for a plebiscite from the Mexican people accepting him as their Emperor, not just the Conservatives – all Mexicans. Forey quickly arranged it. Maximilian also insisted on a signed guarantee from Napoleon III not to recall the Imperial Army until all of Mexico was pacified. The Foreign Legion would also remain. The Paris Accord stipulated economic support although the terms were vague. Mexico was to assume certain debts and obligations and pay the expenses of the invasion as well as the army after his arrival. Maximilian had the verbal support of his father-in-law, Leopold I of Belgian, and at least the approval of his brother, Franz Joseph. Once the Paris Accords were signed, Napoleon sent thirty thousand troops more under the command of one of his toughest strategist, Marshall Bazaine, to quickly pacify Mexico. Maximilian and Carlota set off on a journey through Europe to assist at lavish European balls in their honor, crystal tinkling to toast a new dynasty in America. In spite of the good wishes, Maximilian realized that he depended on France alone for material support and protection.

It was hot and humid that April day in 1864 when Maximilian and Carlota arrived in the port of Veracruz. There was no one to meet them, no bands playing, no triumphal arches nor flowers thrown by joyous citizens. They returned to their ship for dinner. The next day, the President of the Regency, filled with apologies for his late arrival, welcomed them with belated salvos from the fort of San Juan de Ulua. In Spanish, Maximilian addressed "the people": "Mexicans, your noble nation, by a spontaneous majority, has designated me to govern you. With great happiness I submit to that call".

Carlota shivered as she watched buzzards circling, perched on every cornice, a city full of black scavengers and yellow fever. The next day the journey to their new home began. Carlota looked up, up, through palm trees to a snow-capped mountain. They boarded the hot, stuffy train, followed by their retinue of a few noblemen and 100 personal escorts, Hungarian Hussars and French lancers After a short ascent, the railroad ended. Maximilian´s carriage was unloaded and assembled - soon to break a wheel crossing a rough ravine.

The ten-day journey was filled with terrifying and spellbinding experiences: gaudily plumed parrots screeched from thatched roofs as they climbed from trees hung with exotic orchids to coffee plantations then up to pine forests. Adobe huts...white-clad Indians in peaked straw hats and women in bright rebozos… a saphire sky .. unfamiliar scents....so many contrasts seemingly in harmony. A magnificent reception in Puebla, hosted by French officers and the elite loyalists of Puebla and Mexico City.... the next day, winding around the giant sleeping lady volcano on the rutted old "Camino Real" carved out by the Spaniards... then suddenly, the stupendous view of the valley of Anahuac spread out below them. This was where Cortés first saw the city of Tenochitlán. Would he, too, Maximilian wondered, have a short welcome and then only face conflicts?

With all the pomp and ceremony expected of his supporters, Maximilian was crowned in the Cathedral where Iturbide, the first Emperor of Mexico, had been crowned in 1821. Iturbide´s crown was a stage prop, Maximilian´s was to prove a "phantom crown." The new Emperor and his beautiful Empress moved into the lavishly redecorated castle of the Viceroys. Carlota duly selected her ladies-in-waiting from among Mexico´s most notable families and began to learn the ways of the Mexicans. She was fascinated with the native culture and added colorful rebozos to her wardrobe.

Maximilian selected his Cabinet and set about to explore the land, not going beyond the perimeters held by his French troops. In his charro ensembles, short jacket, leather pants split to the knee and big felt hat, he was seen galloping over the mountains to explore a sugar mill or silver mine. His had his picture taken in the dress suit of the charros, tight black pants, jacket, big hat, all adorned with silver braid and buttons. Mexico was penetrating his being as well as his wardrobe. The soft spoken, servile Indians especially touched him. He passed a law returning to them ancestral lands which had been illegally taken by old *hacendados*. Some of the new French *hacendados* complained to no avail. It is said that Maximilian had an Indian lover, La india bonita," in Cuernavaca, his favorite week-end retreat where the beautiful Borda Gardens provided an idyllic paradise.

The first major conflict Maximilian was to face was with the Church. Rome sent out a Nuncio to settle the Church question: Maximilian must declare invalid the laws passed by the infidel Juárez! Invalid! "Absurd", Maximilian replied. He was inspired by the progressive views of the New World and considered himself an enlightened sovereign. The Vatican was attempting to encumber this struggling nation with its medieval despotism. The Church´s feudal holdings he would not restore, nor would he rescind the agreement to permit freedom of worship, at the same time declaring the Catholic faith the religion of the State. As a recompense, Maximilian proposed an agreement in which the State would assume responsibility for the salaries of the clergy.

The Nuncio´s face grew crimson. The rift became acute. Liberals began to praise Maximilian, proclaiming that he had defended the doctrines of Juárez. Monarchists who had placed Maximilian on the throne, derided his anti-Church attitude. The city was divided in open camps, incited by the press. Carlota wrote an angry letter to her friend, Empress Eugenie, Napoleon´s wife: "Our Conservatives regard themselves as retainers of the Pope...to whom religion is synonymous with tithes and the power to hold property!" She gave her full support to her husband.

Carlota stood on the terrace of the castle looking over ancient cypress trees that had existed in the forest of Chapultepec since Moctezuma´s time. She had written to family and friends describing the gardens and fountains she had constructed in this beautiful castle. She felt content here. Built on a high rocky hill, like Miramar, she could see all over the valley of Mexico. The lakes and canals sparkled and the majestic volcanoes seemed so eternal. From the terrace off her bedroom she could see the Palace in the zócalo through her spy glasses and watch Maximilian´s carriage when it drove out through its high portals Her beloved Max had surprised her and had the road cut through all the way to the castle. He had named it "The Emperor´s Drive" and said one day the broad but barren avenue would resemble the Champs Elysée.

On the sixteenth of September, Maximilian journeyed to the town of Dolores Hidalgo and gave a patriotic speech in Spanish, paying homage to "our heroes". On the same day, Benito Juárez gave a passionate speech in the northern state of Chihuahua deriding the usurper and urging volunteers to join his army and overthrow him! Marshall Bazaine took one town after another in the south only to have guerrillas reoccupy them after overcoming the sparse French outposts. The European was unable to foretell the surprise attacks of the enemy, not even his crack black African troops, masters of desert fighting, could cope with the Mexican guerrillas. Carlota was horrified at the sacrifice of young Belgian volunteers whom her father had sent over. She urged Maximilian to demand more French troops. What about the Paris Accord? He did not tell her that the treasury was bankrupt. Juárez held the custom houses on the U.S. border reducing Mexico´s income immeasurably. In the infamous agreement, he had pledged to pay the army´s expenses as well as honor the enormous and inflated French debt. His Foreign Legion had to guard the silver transports that left for Veracruz. And they had spent far more than planned on renovating the castle and entertaining. The Empire had been bled dry by taxes and mere interest payments on the foreign debt. There was no money for educating his gentle underfed Indians, the backbone of his Empire. Juárez must be put down – or join him! Profoundly tolerant and having never subscribed to the archaic, neurotic ethos of the European Courts, Maximilian had soon realized that he sided with the Liberals in their views. He and Juárez held the same visions for a just Mexico, rich and poor united under the law. Together they could make this dream come true! In a flight of fancy, Maximilian formally proposed that Juarez surrender and become Chief Justice of the Supreme Court. The answer was terse: Never! The Republic would continue to fight until the foreign invaders were driven from its shores.

Bazaine incorporated all who were willing of the Conservative Army and soon began to conscript untrained, bewildered Indians who did not understand what they were fighting for. He headed north. Juárez hastily sent a message to his friend, President Lincoln, asking for his full support now to drive out the French. On April 14, shocking news reached his ears. Lincoln had been assasinated! Maximilian hastened to send a confidential messenger with condolences and a proposal for a conference with the new government. President Andrew Jackson dismissed him summarily: the United States recognized Benito Juárez as the legitimate President of Mexico.

Napoleon III was sleepless. His Mexican adventure was not going as anticipated. Not even Bazaine had been able to pacify the country and now Maximilian was in financial trouble. The rumor began circulating that the French Army had invaded that innocent country and taxed the French people to pay the bankers.... Bizmark was on the rise; he had united Germany and it would not be long before he cast his eyes on France. And this morning he had received an unexpected call from the newly appointed American Minister to France who had only one burning question: "What are French troops doing in Mexico?" Thinking fast, Napoleon had replied that they were there to insure payment of the Mexican debt. "And when will they leave?" "Soon," Napoleon snapped tersely. "And who is that Emperor?" "An Austrian Hapsburg who is trying to bring some order to the chaos that is Mexico. With your leave, I have an engagement." Immediately, Napoleon sent a private message to Bazaine. "Start withdrawing your troops. I want them completely out in a year. Do not tell Maximilian." Mexico would not enhance "la gloire de la patrie".

The die was cast. As the French Army began to leave, Mexican guerrillas popped up everywhere to fight for the

Republic. In a hotly contested act, Juárez refused to cede the Presidency to the President of the Supreme Court when his term ended. By a narrow vote, Congress reelected him. This was no time to change Presidents.

It was soon evident to Maximilian and Carlota that Napoleon did not intend to live up to the Paris Accord. The Liberals were taking one city after another and the French forces were embarking for Europe... The end was nearing. Maximilian vacillated: should he renounce his throne and dismiss the loyal Mexicans who were defending him? Carlota cried out "You can´t abdicate! As long as you wear that crown, you are Mexico."

Taking with her evidence of Napoleon´s betrayal, Carlota departed for France; she would demand that Napoleon return his troops! "Napoleon was sick, Napoleon was away, " He refused to receive her. Surrounded by his wife and Ministers, the Emperor of France finally faced the defiant young Empress of Mexico. Her Chamberlain had hardly opened his briefcase when Napoleon´s entire staff was on the defensive, deriding Mexico for its failure to pay, providing reams of lists of the gigantic cost to France her husband was causing. The removal of French troops was justified: Napoleon needed them in France.... Crestfallen, Carlota pleaded with Franz Joseph – not troops, he could not, but diplomatic support, yes. The recurring rumor that the United States threatened to invoke the Monroe Doctrine to drive Maximilian out aroused the indignation of diplomats on both continents. The dictatorial policy of the United States was treating a "Doctrine" as law to oust a government simply because it did not suit them. ...She took her plea to the Vatican but the Church pulled out its long list of grievances against her husband. In growing despair Carlota toured the Capitals of Europe seeking help, becoming every day more agitated, tormented, sometimes raging, accusing her hosts of trying to poison her to get rid of her and let Max die. After months of raving and battling her phantoms she was declared insane and eventually confined to a manor house in Belgian.

Maximilian faced a decisive moment: Juárez´ forces had grown to thirty thousand. Carlota was not present to watch her husband button his uniform and sheath his sword. He would lead his army, six thousand loyal Mexicans and the remaining French. Personally he led a small troop to the City of Querétaro which Juárez was rapidly approaching. Querétaro was in French hands. His able Mexican Generals convinced him that if they could defeat the small advancing Liberal Army they could hold the entrance to Querétaro and defeat Juárez´ hordes.

The plan failed. The siege of Querétaro by Juárez´ overwhelming Army lasted months. Maximilian was imprisoned. As his body shriveled from hunger, so too did his hope for clemency. Juárez, governing from San Luis Potosí, set a date for the execution. The news circled the world. Suddenly this Indian who had risen from the cornfields had become a man of universal importance. From all over the world, Juárez received cablegrams and messengers asking that he spare Maximilian´s life. Every Crown in Europe, Garibaldi who had just unified Italy and was a declared Liberal, the President of the United States and even men of letters like Victor Hugo pleaded for Maximilian´s life. "Let him return to his castle in Miramar. He is not a usurper, not an invader; to his knowledge he was invited by the Mexicans themselves." Napoleon pledged to recall every last soldier. Even Juárez´ own General Escobedo, who had imprisoned Maximilian, tried to convince his President that he would be more respected if he spared the poor Austrian´s life. Juárez stone face showed no emotion. "It is not I who condemn him," he said. "It is the law. It is the will of the people." "Who are these nefarious ´people´" a French newspaper asked. "Two of his Mexican Generals chose to face the firing squad with him and the people of Querétaro fed him and his army during the long siege."

Maximilian was executed on the Hill of Bells in Querétaro on June 20, 1867. His last words were "May my blood flow for the good of this land. Viva Mexico!" He is buried with the Hapsburgs in Vienna. Carlota was told of her husband´s death and in her madness talked to him every day. Hers was to be a long life: five Empires crashed in her time on earth, cannons of the first world war echoed off the walls of her garden, the jazz age was born, automobiles and radio became commonplace and Paris became the Mecca of new cultures – discordant music, distorted painting, sex mentioned on the avant-garde stage. Carlota died in 1927 at the age of 86, an Empress to the end.

The reign of the tragic Emperor and Empress of Mexico lasted only three years but has inspired countless books, a play, a movie. Their presence in Mexico is now enshrined in the Castle of Chapultepec, today a museum. Maximilian´s magnificent golden carriage is on prominent display. The personal quarters of the Emperor and Empress of Mexico are visited by people from all over the world. Many stand on Carlota´s terrace and marvel at the view of tall buildings along a broad, tree-lined avenue traced by Maximilian and called "Paseo de la Reforma," Avenue of the Reform in honor of Benito Juárez. Juarez´ black carriage can be seen in the same room as Maximilian´s carriage.

Maximilian´s last bastion, Puebla, fell to the Liberal Army of Porfirio Díaz. Marching down the mountain singing victory, Díaz soon reached Mexico City. With a well-executed strategy, his army of 35000 surrounded the Capital and forced the remaining French and Conservatives to hastily depart. At sunset, Juárez´ black carriage drove into the Capital where the defender of the Constitution again took his rightful seat. He had survived ten years of conflict.[30]

The triumph of the Republic brought to a closure the long struggle for independence championed by Hidalgo and Morelos. 1867 marked the end of an epoch. Mexico was now constituted as a federal, representative and lay government. And so it has remained. Like all historical heroes, they become myths, legends in history books, the black marks seldom recounted. It has been noted that Benito Juárez signed the infamous McLane-Ocampo treaty in which Mexico sold to the United States the right of passage by rail from the Pacific to the Gulf of Mexico across the Isthmus of Tehuantepec, guarded by American troops with free entry into Mexico. The railroad was started but fortunately, the treaty was not ratified by the United States Congress. Numerous times, in his desperation to

30 Zuloaga´s Conservative government, which occupied the Palace, was recognized first by the United States, but when he declined to sell more land than specified in the Maclain-Ocampo treaty, the U.S. favored Juarez, the Liberal President still fighting the Conservative Army.

raise funds "to save the Republic", Juárez was tempted to sell Baja California and a portion of Chihuahua and Sonora to the United States. It did not come to pass. He has been accused of using the Constitution as a veil to hide his reelections. But the fact of what he accomplished, his honesty and integrity, his unbending resolve to defend the Republic to the death, has placed his name high on the roster of Mexican heroes. There is a " Juárez" street in almost every town in Mexico. A magnificent white marble hemicycle graces Alameda Park in downtown Mexico City. His words, "With individuals, as with nations, the respect for the rights of others is peace" are engraved in stone, bronze and marble. Benito Juárez was re-elected again in 1871 and died in office in 1872.

Mexico was still not destined to enjoy peace. In Juárez´ last term, the internal debt had grown to astronomical figures and the English were still beating at the door of Congress. But industry and commerce had begun to pick up. Climbing 10,000 feet from the Gulf coast, the spectacular railroad from Veracruz to Mexico City, started in 1850, was finally inaugurated in 1873. A well-developed textile industry was growing. Mines began to operate with new equipment. Most imports and exports were in foreign hands – half of it British. Contraband through the Pacific coast harbors had kept money flowing into the hands of local merchants for years, unhampered by the government. Foreign arms contractors had moved tons of arms through these ports as ships had sailed up and down the unwatched Pacific coast. In mid century, many passengers, infected with "gold fever", had crossed over through Panama, then ship to California to join the mad "gold rush". Sailing up and down they bought and sold every manner of goods in Mexico´s ports without paying taxes. Juárez had finally established customs´ houses in the principal ports of Manzanillo, Mazatlán and Acapulco which had added to much needed revenue. But in 1869 the completion of the transcontinental railroad in the United States eliminated the active commerce in Mexico´s Pacific ports.

Juárez initiated the building of new schools, new roads and the repair of churches but the rumble of discontent echoed across canyons and sounded off village walls. The old caciques no longer had guerrillas to lead nor had they been given political positions or recompense for their victories. Soldiers had been dismissed to return to bleak homes without pay. The country was soon infested with bandits who raided the commercial routes and made travel dangerous. Only the stout hearted rode the stagecoaches, escorted by soldiers, – seven days east to Veracruz, thirteen days west to Guadalajara, a month north to Monterrey. Juárez´ dream of a country of small landholders and a prosperous middle class had died in the three years of civil war. Indians who had worked old communal lands had been given deeds to their parcels but they had soon been seduced by mestizos who bought their deeds for a pittance. Unlike colonial days, many new hacendados were the children of foreigners who had worked for corporations and factories which had been confiscated under La Ley Lerdo; they had paid the land taxes and obtained legal deeds to their haciendas. This new breed of creoles of French, German, British and American descent would carry political and economic weight in the future.

While Texans were driving cattle down from as far north as Canada and populating their state, Mexico´s population had been decimated by war and disease. The mortality rate was grim; hunger and little knowledge of hygiene were endemic problems of the poor. Cantinas multiplied as the male population got drunk on five centavos of *pulque* or *aguardiente*. Constant upheaval and uncertainty had taken much of Mexico´s foreign capital and talent to Argentina, Venezuela, Chile, even Brazil. Mexico had come to be known as "the land of eternal revolution". Although by 1872 Mexico City was the largest in all Latin America[31] with a population of nearly 300,000, it was a city in disrepair, a city whose history had been pounded down in cobblestone streets and undulating sidewalks through the generations. Like a veil, weariness and discontent covered the country when Juárez died. Discontent vexed the Congress.

Sebastián Lerdo de Tejada became interim President following Juárez´ death, then ran for office in 1876 – and won in a bitterly contested election.[32] The undisputed leader of the discontented Liberals was Porfirio Díaz. A handsome, astute, fearless fighter from Oaxaca, he had fought in seventy battles since he was seventeen. It was he who had supported Zaragoza against the French invaders in the first battle of Puebla on that famous May 5th, he who had placed the Capital under siege and forced Maximilian´s Conservatives to hastily depart. He had opened the way

31 In 1861 the term Latin America was quoted for the first time in the French press. France, not being present in America at the time, wanted to strengthen the Latin culture in this continent.

32 The Laws of the Reform,were added to the Constitution during the presidency of Lerdo De Tejada (1872-1876).

for Juárez to return. Juárez , himself, had raised his rank to General. In the last election he had run against his former law professor shouting "Dictator! It is not the Constitution he defends but his seat in the Presidential chair. No reelection!" Juárez warned Congress that Porfirio Díaz was an ambitious and dangerous man. In an attempted coup Díaz was defeated and returned to Oaxaca. When Lerdo de Tejado was elected for a second term in 1876, Diaz was prepared. In a blistering coup, Lerdo was forced to abandon the struggle and left in self exile. His career as a soldier had molded Diaz into the tough, crafty, forceful dictator who was to rule Mexico for the next thirty-three years.

CHAPTER XIII

In his heart, Porfirio Díaz respected and admired Benito Juárez. Both came from Oaxaca, one a pure zapotec, the other of mixteca blood, both enigmatic, paternal Presidents who shared a deep love of country. They also shared the same vision of a peaceful, modern, prosperous Mexico. Juárez had established the basis: the law. He achieved political stability. Now it was up to the new generation to achieve economic stability.

After Lerdo left in self-imposed exile and Díaz´ presidency was legally ratified by Congress, he focused all his political and military acumen in one direction: Peace, Order and Progress. They were engraved on his brain. Peace was of the first order – at any price. To combat banditry, Díaz created a corps of *Rurales*, bandit leaders turned rural police, well mounted and well paid. Thieves catching thieves. Riding in their charro uniforms with their big felt hats, the feared *Rurales* kicked up dust in every remote village. They knew all the tricks and hiding places of those they now pursued leaving a chain of bodies hanging from trees in their wake. In four years the countryside and the roads were safe.

His long career as a soldier had taught Díaz that armies were built on obedience to authority. His was to be an absolute authority. Tactical warfare required a well-coordinated strategy: applied to politics - make your enemy believe he has you in a corner, then yank out the rug. Pit one contender against another without disclosing which you intend to support. Ambivalence kept all sides guessing: show seeming favoritism to one political aspirant while fanning the ambition of another. Soon they would start to destroy each other. Carry a fire extinguisher and a balancing rod to keep the political factions under control. He generously distributed cabinet positions among the different factions and favors among former enemies until there was no opposition. Wisely, Díaz chose men of experience, intelligent men. "Bread and the stick" for the military: concessions – mines and land was the bread offered in return for absolute loyalty - menacing accusations, shame, ostracism for those who did not obey. To insure against new guerrilla uprisings, Díaz formed a well-equipped, well-trained National Army and sent its officers to France and England to be trained. A local police force kept the city streets free of robberies….Control of the press: "tighten the rein but don´t let it snap." Conciliation with the Church was necessary: discreetly ignoring the anti-church legislation of the Constitution, Diaz permitted entry to new missionaries and educators. Parochial schools reopened. In return, the Church ordered the faithful to obey civil authority. A 33 degree Mason, Diaz presided over Masonic ceremonies, maintained excellent relationships with the Protestants at the same time declaring himself a faithful Catholic. He was a master of the art of seduction.

Crafty and despotic he has been called. But his "big stick" offered peace and stability. After fifty years of fighting, people were willing to submit to the will of a dictator. Before the end of his first term Diaz had obtained the recognition of the United States as President of the Republic of Mexico. Diligently, he had paid every installment on the foreign debt.

Honoring his battle cry of "Effective suffrage. No reelection!" Diaz chose his compadre and companion in war, Manuel Gonzalez, to run for office in 1880. With his puppet safely installed, Díaz returned to Oaxaca where he served as Governor. The Constitution allowed reelection after an intervening term so in 1884, Diaz returned to the Capital and won with a commanding majority. As had happened with Juárez and Lerdo, the restriction of the Constitution placed a brake on his personal agenda. In 1887, Diaz expanded the Constitutional clause on reelection to allow indefinite reelection. An election was rigorously held every four years but became, in effect, a farce, a ritual to the cult of the strong man, the man who brought order, peace and progress to Mexico.

Carmelita Romero Rubio put her books down on the small table and awaited her pupil with a fast-beating heart. She had been schooled in a Catholic convent in the United States and was a proficient English teacher. Carmelita dressed in the latest fashion, held her head high like the aristocrat she was and spoke in well-modulated tones. She was seventeen, the daughter of an important politician linked to the rich groups of central Mexico, a rich man himself, and a force in the Lerdo government. Carmelita was intrigued by her pupil, quite rough around the edges but he exuded determination, self-confidence – and a masculine power she sensed in military men. He was also a bit frightening. A widower for more than a year, he was the talk of female gatherings and ambitious mothers. Carmelita stood up and straightened her skirt when she heard him approach. Porfirio Díaz entered the study and wished his young teacher a good day… Before the year´s end, in 1881, a Catholic priest united Carmen Romero Rubio, seventeen, with Porfirio Díaz, fifty-one. He had acquired a polished jewel and she a rough diamond ready to be polished under her tutelage.

The last decade of the century was a decade of opulence. "Don Porfirio," as he was affectionately called, reigned in the Republic and was recognized abroad as an illustrious statesman. Carmelita had converted the rough soldier into a well-polished gentleman. She cut his beard, bought him gloves, hired tailors, taught him that it was incorrect to spit on the floor, taught him English and took him to Europe, a Europe enjoying its "Belle Epoque"

The U.S had consolidated its march west, a march matched by the rapid advance of technology: the light bulb, the phonograph, the telephone, the airplane and the automobile greeted the XX century. In the United States, railroads connected Texas with Canada, New York with San

Francisco while in Mexico a scarce six hundred kilometers of track had been laid. . Diaz had met Thomas Edison in New York and avidly followed the latest inventions. Eager to modernize communication, Díaz had installed the first telephone lines as early as 1879 and expanded telegraph connections. By the end of his second term, 1888, Díaz had opened the gates wide to foreign investors.

Since the1880s Europe had been busy dividing up Africa. England had acquired a vast Empire and now, with her colonies firmly established, looked across the Atlantic to Mexico. Veracruz was filled with ships from all over the globe – the most prevalent flags those of England, France and Germany, but the flags of Italy, Spain, Holland and Japan also waved from mastheads. In spite of the uproar by the Americans, Díaz granted Japan fishing rights in the Gulf of Cortés off the coast of Baja California.

Once the west was won, the new Manifest Destiny of the United States was commercial conquest. The United States now looked upon Mexico as a supplier of natural resources: silver, gold, copper, lead, lumber, grazing lands, cheap labor. In 1900 an American wildcatter, Edward Doheney, drilled a hole in the ground in Tampico and a sticky black substance, known to the Indians, exploded from the earth, a gusher of black gold. Oil! The English were right behind the Americans and it would not be long before the Lord of the Admiralty, Winston Churchill, convinced Parliament to convert the British Navy from coal to oil. Weetman Pearson, the English engineer who had constructed the railroad that traversed the Isthmus of Tehuantepec, joining the Pacific with the Gulf of Mexico, was a favorite of Don Porfirio. Díaz granted Pearson the most favorable oil contract for which the engineer was conferred with the Royal title of Lord Cowdry. The Shell Oil Company of England and the U.S. Standard Oil Company struck gusher after gusher.

Politically, Díaz, controlled every office in the land. He "voted in" the Governors, the Mayors and Congress. *"El Dedazo"*, finger-pointing was enough; he simply pointed a finger at a candidate and the man was elected. Francisco Bulnes, an intellectual and historian states the nation´s condition in few words: "Progress, credit and peace depend upon Porfirio Díaz. Porfirio Díaz is mortal. Progress, credit and peace will die with him." Economic progress was well sealed but social progress was stagnant.

What festered was the land issue. Like Carlos III, in the XVIII century, who had sent his top administrator to audit every enterprise, stop corruption and turn New Spain into a more productive possession, Díaz ignored the social problems in his march of Progress. The peon was again a virtual slave on the haciendas which had encroached and encroached to swallow up villages. The land was in the hands of a few. The Terraza family of Chihuahua joked that their haciendas were not in the State of Chihuahua, Chihuahua was in their estate. Americans owned huge tracts of land – the Guggenheims and Rockefellers in the northeast; Hearst owned three million hectares in the northwest. Enormous fortunes were made. "The Mexican can endure oppression, servility and tyranny," Díaz told an American reporter, "what he fears is the lack of bread, lack of a roof, and the need to sacrifice the fiesta for lack of means." In simplistic terms food, family and fiesta were the pillars of life. They were sufficient for the populacho.

*The day dawned clear and beautiful for the tradi-
tional spring "battle of flowers". The Alameda Park had
been cordoned off for the event and the populace strained
against the ropes to catch a good look at the beautiful
carriages. In the grandstand, tall silk hats and derbies
stood out in a sea of flowered dresses and floppy hats
that hid the expectant feminine faces. In the front row
the judges sat in solemn file. The carriages lined up, a
display of roses, magnolias, daisies, gladiolas -every kind
of flower -draped in swags around the open carriages.
Young society girls in ruffled dresses with big bows in
their hair held the reins of their ponies or horses which
had just strutted around the park showing off their
young contestants. Troubadours played their guitars
and a hundred violins serenaded them. Finally, the
Marshall raised his trumpet and quieted the crowd. The
winner was announced: "First place - Señorita María
Alicia Corcuera y Escalante." The Queen of the Fairies
with her myriad clusters of roses, paper butterflies and
greenery led the procession to Chapultepec Park where
they threw flowers at each other and a stream of little
urchins followed them gleefully picking up the flowers
and throwing them back. That night the Queen of the
Fairies slept the sleep of the enchanted.*

*In their one-room adobe hut, Juana squatted on
her knees before her brasero patting out tortillas and
laying them on the hot comal as had her mother and
her grandmother and her grandmother´s grandmother.
The smoke rose through the kitchen lean-to without*

disturbing the baby who slept in a small hammock hung from the roof. Juana sat back for a minute and held her stomach. Was she pregnant again? Two children had died before they were a year old, maybe this one would die too. She heard Tomás approaching and resumed her task. It was nearly dusk. He had left at dawn as usual. Tomás sank down on the dirt floor. "Find Carlos," she said "and tell him to go for water." Carlos was eleven and could now carry two buckets. The nearest well was a kilometer away. "And tell Antonio to gather more fire wood. I am nearly out. The boys are outside", she finished. Tomás got up and stretched his weary back. "I will go with Antonio. He can't carry an armful yet." Antonio was five. After the family had eaten their tacos of frijoles, nopales, and rice, Juana spread her rebozo over the two boys and lay down beside Tomás. He was too tired to even turn over. She said the rosary before going to sleep and thanked God for the sack of rice the "Patrona", wife of the hacendado, had sent her.

The general public napped in peace and dreamed of material well-being. As though they had been hypnotized by some sorcerer, they looked only within their walls and within their own family. The nation was at peace. The treasury was full. Abroad, Díaz had earned an international reputation as the Savior of Mexico, the man who honored his debts and honored his contracts. At home, he was the tlatoani , the Viceroy, the Royal President, a stern but benevolent father. In the first decade of the XX century, Díaz´ mania for "Progress" infiltrated the political ranks whose leaders began to be known as "los científicos", the scientists.

They were convinced that technology was going to save the world – especially Mexico. Instead of the smoke of cannons, the smoke of 5500 factories dotted the landscape. Textile mills, glass factories, steel and paper, cement, soap, shoes, beer and cigarettes, were all being manufactured in Mexico. Mexico was the fifth producer of gold in the world, the second in copper and the first in silver.

Mexicans were showing an aptitude for tools. Capable foremen were being trained. American engineers, architects, cattle ranchers, miners, railroad men, factory owners were training and employing thousands of Mexicans, albeit their wages were a pittance compared to American workers and only a few pesos dribbled into the national coffers from the low taxes they paid. The danger was that Yankee investors now dominated both exports and imports. Díaz famous statement, "Poor Mexico, so far from God and close to the United States" echoed loudly. "When they sneeze up there," he also said, "we catch pneumonia." To maintain a balance among investors, Díaz courted Europe. In his cunning, he kept a pawn on his chess board which sorely irritated the United States. Whenever his northern neighbor began dictating policy to him, he let it be known he was considering selling Baja California to the Japanese.

From the beginning, Díaz had realized that the greatest hindrance to progress was lack of transportation. A nation with little contact among its regions is a nation without cohesion. Railroads and bridges were of prime importance. The Americans and English had vied with each other to lay track but the English bowed to the Americans as the mines and oil became their prime interests. William Randolph Hearst hastened to continue the route of his Pacific Railway from California down through Mexico. At the beginning of the XX century, railroads were becoming the lifeblood of the nation, uniting north with south, the Gulf with the Pacific, winding through the rugged mountains that for centuries had separated Mexicans from each other and Mexico into isolated pockets. During Diaz´ long regime, 19,280 kilometers of track were laid. Fearing an American monopoly, as had happened when Standard Oil controlled the shipping line that connected Veracruz with New Orleans and New York, in 1908, Ives Limantour, Díaz´ astute Secretary of the Treasury, fused all railroad lines into one company under majority Mexican capital. The Mexican National Railway was hailed as a great achievement by Mexicans who had developed a proud sense of "Nation" and began to resent the favorable position of the foreigners in Mexico.

Since colonial times, the bullfight had been the principal diversion of the population; the sound of the trumpet sent an electrifying surge around the ring as the bull charged out from the tunnel. Circuses and country fairs with their Ferris wheels and carousels had never stopped traveling from town to town. In the smallest village, the fiesta to the patron saint was the maximum diversion. Now foreigners offered new challenges to the old diversions introducing the fun and excitement of sports. They were promoting tennis, basket ball, bicycle riding, athletic clubs, boxing, horse-racing, soccer-football, baseball, even an elegant Country Club with an eighteen-hole golf course. An avowed exercise devotee, Porfirio Díaz encouraged athletic events and brought the YMCA to Mexico. The British had introduced the game of cricket as early as 1827 and British miners in Pachuca had taught their workers to play "futbol", the origin of today´s number one national sport. American railroad workers were teaching their Mexican colleagues to play baseball, a game which caught on especially in the northern states. Introduced by Americans in Cuba in 1860, word reached Mexico that the game drew crowds of thousands and Cuban teams were competing in the United States. In 1895, the Mexican Baseball club defeated the champions, the American Baseball Club, a feat that made headlines in the press. Sporting goods stores that sold tennis shoes, bicycles, saddles, all manner of equipment soon sprang up. Don Porfirio built an elegant race track which ladies could attend and the Jockey Club was established in one of Mexico´s most historic buildings, the house of tiles in downtown Mexico City.[33] Free tickets to many events kept the populace happy. But it was the bullfight that told the truth about the division of classes: the ring was divided into "Sun" and "Shade". "Shade" cost three times as much and cushions were provided for its occupants.

Díaz viewed education as essential to achieve progress and national unity. The illiteracy rate was 85 percent. Justo Sierra, his brilliant Minister of Education, said: "More than half the inhabitants of this Republic ignore what it means to be Mexican, to be part of the national conscience. The misery of their circumstance and means of life, the predominance of superstition and alcoholism prevents contact with the soul of the nation. It is indispensable, it is urgent, it is urgently indispensable that within two generations

33 Today, this unique 18th century bulding houses the original Sanborns´store.

this state of affairs be modified….. With our schools let us open windows everywhere to the outside air, to the air of our Nation, to the air of human civilization. Let us not waste a day, let us not waste an hour in this sacred task." Secular, free, compulsory education, written into law by Juárez, was reinforced. The object was to fuse white, mestizo and indigenous children into educated, useful Mexicans. During the Díaz regime ten thousand primary schools were built, the quality of education better than the private schools – mostly Catholic. Hygiene was incorporated into the curriculum. One out of every two children in Mexico were dying of infections like pneumonia and diarrhea before the age of five. Boiling water, washing hands, warmer clothes were the antidotes.

Foreigners and city-Mexicans alike considered Indians dirty, backward, submissive, apathetic. It occurred to only a few that they were apathetic because they were hungry; they were dirty because they had little access to water. To lift them out of this mire would be a continuing challenge. The first barrier was the campesino father. Education was of no importance to him; his children were needed to help plant, to water the fields, to harvest the small family parcel. Rural schools were few, difficult to reach and often without a teacher. The cities offered adult educational programs which included technical schools for both men and women: carpentry, blacksmithing, mechanical workshops for the men, typing, pattern- making, sewing, even photography for the women. The few who achieved higher education - engineers, doctors, lawyers, architects – competed with the best but foreign employers considered them less capable than their own people.

In the last decade of his dictatorship, Díaz focused on converting the Capital into a magnificent European style city. He was consumed with preparing for the great Centennial celebration of Independence to take place in 1910. Foreign architects and engineers flocked to Mexico to compete for the ambitious government projects: a Legislative Palace to be compared with the Capitol in Washington, a marble Opera House, remodeling the old University buildings, a new Insane Asylum, a Telegraph building, an imposing marble Hemicycle to honor Benito Juárez in the Alameda Park, an Independence monument in one of the circles that marked the elegant Paseo de la Reforma, Maximilian´s dream of a Champs Elysée come true. Mexican professionals had to fight for recognition; Public Works did not consider them competent although they may have earned their degree in Paris. Never had there been such a frenzy of work since Cortés built the Capìtal of New Spain. A visiting Mexican who had lived abroad for ten years remarked: "When I left, Mexico was a city of peeling walls, foul odors and potholes that could break an axle. Now it´s a city of barricades, gaping holes, gigantic machines and dust. I haven´t seen the volcanoes in weeks."

Stagnant waters still mired the streets. After a thunderstorm, downtown Mexico City seemed like a swamp. For fifty centavos an Indian would carry a shopper on his back to the other side of the street. Díaz contracted American engineers who channeled off the remaining water of the lakes and installed a modern drainage system. The discovery of an enormous round stone lost among the ruins of Tenochtitlán created a sensation. It was identified as the Aztec calendar.

The transformation of the city into "the Paris of the western hemisphere" was underway. Crumbling colonial buildings were torn down and cobblestone streets torn up by giant American steam shovels while flocks of turkeys tried to avoid being trampled as they were driven to market along the old routes. History had crawled along those streets, now American steamrollers were laying new history in asphalt. Automobiles honked loudly causing horses to buck as they were suddenly reined in. Santa Anna´s National Theater was torn down to open the area where a magnificent neo-classic marble Opera House was under construction. The Opera house (today the Palace of Fine Arts called Bellas Artes) and a regal Post Office, reminiscent of a Venetian palace, was the work of the renowned Italian architect, Adamo Boari. Electric trams replaced mule-drawn trolleys and the main streets had electric lights. Fashionable stores had tempting displays of clothing, jewelry and articles from around the world – in particular France. France was the font of culture, all things French were in vogue – Paris hats and Paris gowns set the style, gilded furniture filled the homes of the rich and classic statuary adorned public buildings. The growing middle class copied every design. Relegated to native markets and curio shops, Mexican crafts were considered "vulgar". Colorful pottery, blown-glass animals and dressed fleas, encased in a hollow walnut shell and sealed under glass, were favorite "curios" of the tourists. In elegant restaurants the patron could dine on gourmet dishes and the finest wines. "The French own the textile mills and the department stores, the Germans the pharmacies and hardware stores, the Spanish the bakeries and grocery stores, the Italians the foundries and marble works, the Americans and English own the factories, the railroads and the oil fields. What does the Mexican own?" disgruntled underpaid professionals began to ask?

In 1903, Díaz' Ministers and creditors brought up a touchy subject: who would succeed him? Foreign investors were edgy – suppose he suddenly died like Juárez? Díaz was seventy-three. There were already plots to overthrow him. A group of radical Liberals in the city of San Luis Potosí, headed by the Flores Magón brothers, were gaining followers. Clandestine newspapers had been discovered accusing Díaz of violating the rights of States and Municipal Governments. The Constitution was dead prose, they stated. To those caught and locked up in jail, Díaz applied La Ley Fuga: open the cell door, force the prisoner out and shoot him "trying to escape." To ameliorate the fear of his Ministers and creditors, Diaz created the office of Vice-President in time for the election of 1904 and extended the Presidential term to six years. The election in 1910 would coincide with the great Centennial celebration. He would be alive. Yes, he would, he would be very much alive!

Díaz rose at six o'clock, worked out at the gym and took a cold shower as was his daily habit. As he had changed the image of his country, so his personal image had also changed. His skin had gotten whiter, his back straighter. Always a handsome man, he was now the epitome of an imposing aristocrat. Carmelita joined him for breakfast in the private dining room of their suite in the Castle, their summer residence. She was dressed in riding clothes prepared to take their morning canter through the forest of giant cypress trees of Chapultepec Park. She looked at her husband. "What is wrong, Porfirio?" "Nothing," he replied. "You look pale and worried." "I am all right, I tell you." She looked at him unable to read his expression. One of his Ministers had described him exactly: "Always perfectly in character, without smiling, sitting straight as a ramrod, without revealing pleasure or displeasure in his enigmatic expression. He is the perfect sphinx." She loved him and loved her position as "Doña Carmelita", the great man′s perfectly groomed perfectly mannered wife. She would take his temperature tonight to see whether it was something physical.

In 1908 a small book was circulating around the country. It was titled "The Presidential Succession" and examined carefully the existing situation should the President die. In essence the little book said: "Upon the disappearance from the political scene of General Porfirio Díaz, there would be an immediate reaction in favor of democratic principals which guarantee the vote to which all citizens have a right…. I hoped Díaz had changed when he instituted the office of Vice President and convoked a Convention of his so-called Nationalist party. But he imposed his choice for the office without listening to the voices in opposition. The Convention was a farce. As his candidate, Díaz imposed the unpopular, disliked Mr.Ramón Corral who sold the Yaqui Indians of the north in slavery to the plantations of Yucatán. Corral is the official choice….I then understood that we cannot expect any changes when General Díaz disappears because his successor, imposed upon the Republic, will be a man chosen by him" The book implied that for citizens to re-conquer their rights, they might have to resort to arms.

The author of "The Presidential Succession" was Francisco Madero, a wealthy rancher from the northern state of Coahuila. He was the son of a well-connected and respected family who had investments all over Mexico. It bothered Díaz that he was not a poor rebel whom he could put in prison. Two years later he found an excuse.

By 1910, Mexico City had been converted into a European-style Capital.

But the shadows of the trees trembled upon the sidewalks. The social problems festered openly. Cortés' bones rattled in his crypt in the Hospital of Jesus near the Zócalo. It was laughter that made his bones rattle, laughter at the soldier turned dictator. He had permitted his polished Republic to revert the land to the old feudal system in a modern world.

Punctually, at 11:00 p.m. on September 15, the venerable Patriarch, wearing the sash of the Republic, stepped onto the central balcony of the Palace and, standing straight as a ramrod, faced the human mass in the Zócalo who tooted horns and waved little Mexican flags in expectation of the "Grito". Don Porfirio firmly grasped the cord and rang the deep-toned bell of Dolores Hidalgo. "Viva Hidalgo!" he shouted. "Vivaaaaaa!!" resonated as one voice from the Zócalo. "Viva the Heroes of the Independence!" "Vivaaaaa!!" "Viva Mexico!!" Another "Vivaaaa" thundered back. Fireworks burst upon the night sky in dazzling colors. Mariachis played and troubadours sang to him under the balcony. Tears in his eyes, Díaz stepped back from the balcony and proceeded to the Salon of Ambassadors where he received a hundred elite guests gathered to toast his eightieth birthday.

Little boys climbed trees, hung from windows and gaped as the great Parade began. "With a burst of cymbals the military bands struck up. Wave upon wave of sailors and soldiers from around the world rounded the Zócalo and disappeared down the parade route followed by the Mexican Military cadets goose-stepping with precision. The applause was deafening when the charros pranced by in their silver trappings, dazzling the visitors. The bandy-legged old Spanish General, the Marqués de Polavieja, wearing the sash of King Carlos III, marched in front of a cannon displaying the personal effects of Morelos, hero of the Independence, captured and executed by the Royalists in 1815, now returned from their long repository in the Armory of Madrid. The crowd wept and cheered wildly. The French envoy returned the keys to Mexico City, keys given to Marshall Forey by a defeated Mexican army in 1863. Fraternal sentiment ran high when the French saluted the Mexican flag."

On the morning of September 16,1910, the Grand old "Man of the Americas" inaugurated the Statue to Independence. In flawless marble, the figures of the heroes clustered around the tall column. Four imposing bronze female figures flanked the four corners of the base symbolizing Justice, Peace, War and the Law. At the top, Victory spread her wings, holding a broken chain in one hand and a laurel wreath in the other. Every eye looked up at the golden "angel" floating in the sky while a boys´ choir sang the national anthem.

At dawn, the bell of the little church on the hacienda clanged loud and long to summon the workers to their daily meeting. Standing in the arch of the central patio, the administrator assigned the group heads their duties for the day: which fields to harvest, which to plow, cattle to pasture, horses to groom, bulls to test, cows to milk and all the sundry tasks that kept the hacienda alive and productive. It was known to all that the Patrón was off to the city with one of his many mistresses. A day without his harassment and punishment was welcome. The foremen dispersed to meet with their peones.

After morning prayers, after the house staff had received their orders, Doña Clarita moved to the warm patio to embroider. "What are you working on now, Mamá" her seven year old daughter asked. "A pillow, mi hijita. Now run along." She did not say that she was embroidering her sorrows and fears. Busy fingers and the songs of her canaries helped to suppress them. She knew the philandering of her husband, the way he mercilessly worked his peones, the "purchase" of peasant lands that incorporated their village into his estate. Why could not Alfonso treat them like their neighbor, Don Ignacio? Don Ignacio provided doctor, priest, food, water and piñatas for the children at Christmastime. No wonder Alfonso's men deserted to work over there. He had vowed to throw Don Ignacio in prison. "Those peones are indebted to me!" he ranted. "They owe money to the hacienda store as will their sons and their son's sons. They are debtors. They cannot move off this hacienda!" Doña Clarita removed a handkerchief from her sleeve and wiped her eyes. The only people who were free to move from that miserable village were the midwife, the horticulturist who was planting the new orchard, the carpenter, the shoemaker and the artisans. They moved from village to village. The peones might as well have chains. It was an unjust world. She sensed the unrest that lay just below the surface but she could do nothing but pray and stitch her fears into flowers with trembling fingers.

Two French ships lay in Veracruz harbor waiting for their cargo to be unloaded. Soon huge grappling hooks lifted cases of wine, cognac, champagne, boxes of crystal glasses, dinner sets of fine china, tablecloths, tables, chairs, while French waiters and cooks walked down the gangplank.

The great Centennial Ball of 1910 had all the aspects of a Royal celebration.

Fifty thousand bulbs lighted the historic buildings around the Zócalo. A huge sign flashed the words "Paz y Progreso". The crowd pushed and shoved to get a glimpse of the line of carriages and automobiles that discharged their passengers at the gates to the Palace, a fashion show for the gaping populace. Welcoming heads of State from around the world, Don Porfirio and his young wife, Doña Carmelita, wearing a diamond tiara, graciously shook hands as they ushered their guests into the polished reception areas. Every important figure in Mexico was also welcomed by the regal couple including oil barons, architects, artists and business men especially invited for the occasion.

Never had Díaz felt so fulfilled. The world had acknowledged his accomplishments. For thirty-three years he had governed Mexico, accomplishing his goal of peace, order and progress. With the blessing of God and the help of a new, young legislature, he might continue. In the balcony across from them a thirty piece orchestra was playing a waltz. Díaz placed his arm around Carmelita´s waist and started the dancing....

Around the corner, a crowd was marching toward the Zócalo shouting "Muera Díaz" (death to Díaz) and carrying a banner that emblazoned the words, "Viva Madero". Díaz did not know that he was dancing on a volcano.

CHAPTER XIV

"David confronting Goliath" Francisco Madero has been described by many. He was a small man but well-built with tremendous stamina. Like most northern families who had a history of fighting off Apache and Yaqui raids, the Maderos were people of strong character. They were also known for their open-mindedness, honesty and fair treatment of their peones who were paid a fair salary and could move at will. Good ranch hands were scarce in the north and many preferred to cross over to the United States where they were paid more. Francisco Madero maintained a personal contact with his laborers. He was often seen with his homeopathic satchel in hand visiting a sick peon. He provided breakfast and schooling for their children.

The Maderos were from the state of Coahuila which borders on the United States. They were a large clan headed by a Patriarch, Don Evaristo, whose sagacity in business had made them wealthy: silver mines, banks, cattle ranches, henequen plantations in Yucatán and cotton plantations in the north, investments in steel, the leather industry, vineyards and myriad smaller investments brought them in contact with the foreign community and government officials. They were liked and trusted. Francisco was the eldest of twelve, a man with a quick smile who loved to dance the polka. He had attended commercial school in Paris and studied agriculture at the University of California. Impressed with the example of what a democratic state can accomplish, he was convinced that Mexico must be governed democratically for all its people to have equal opportunity. Díaz had deprived them of their vote. They must have a voice. His little book, "The Presidential Succession", published in 1909, had dusted off dormant minds and made his name known throughout the country.

In the famous "Creelman interview" of 1908, Diaz had expressed his opinions and plans to an American reporter more openly than he ever had to the press before. In the interview, he defended his dictatorship: In essence, he said,"When I took over the presidency, there was not a cent in the treasury, the country was deep in debt and lawlessness reigned in the countryside. How could I govern democratically when Mexicans are not democratic minded? They ignore the law, defend their own rights but not the rights of others. An iron fist was necessary. But the purpose of my dictatorship has been to guide Mexico along the path to democracy. Now", he added, "I believe Mexico is prepared for democracy and I will step down in 1910."

The Creelman interview was intended only for foreign consumption but a year later it leaked over the border from the United States, escaped Diaz´ censors and created a blazing headline; "EXTRA. EXTRA. DIAZ DECLARES HE WILL RESIGN IN 1910!" It may have been his intention, but as the 1910 election approached he was caught between two candidates whom he had pitted against each other; each important men with a strong following. It was Diaz´ habit to undermine any faction that had grown powerful – so the only solution was to reelect himself.

Francisco had had several interviews with Díaz, politely but firmly expressing his position only to be scoffed at and described as a crazy young man. In 1909 Madero decided to revive a long ignored party, the Antireelectionists, and traveled to all the major cities forming clubs and naming leaders. In early 1910 a convention was held which elected Francisco Madero as its Presidential candidate. Suddenly Díaz saw a red flag. After a passionate campaign speech in Monterrey, Madero was arrested on grounds of inciting a rebellion and put in jail in the city of San Luis Potosí. There, he wrote a declaration inciting the nation to rise in arms against the dictator on November twentieth, 1910. "I have done everything possible to reach an agreement. I was even willing to withdraw my candidacy if General Díaz had permitted the nation to choose, at the very least, a Vice-President to succeed him. But dominated by incomprehensible pride, he turned a deaf ear upon the nation and preferred to precipitate a revolution." Disguised as a railroad worker, Madero escaped on the central railway to San Antonio, Texas, where his brothers and supporters joined him.

What caused Madero to issue his famous call to arms is a theme historians like to deliberate. Madero was defending the right to vote not social causes. Did he have any idea of what he would stir up? Yes, Mexico needed young men who understood democracy. Madero appealed to them. In a popular newspaper, a cartoon depicted Díaz and his Cabinet as mummies sitting up in their coffins. Francisco's young brother, Julio, declared: " Francisco is a pacifist. He hates violence. But he hates injustice more." In the city of Puebla on November 20th, 1910, the first martyr of the Revolution was killed by Federal forces. Aquiles Serdán´s name has gone down in history as a hero.

The Revolution got off to an anemic start. Madero had escaped to San Antonio, Texas, on a freight train. On February thirteenth, 1911, he crossed the border into Mexico with a small band of armed volunteers. After a few successful skirmishes against weak Federal forces he was joined by Pancho Villa and Pascual Orozco, one a bandit, the other a muleteer, both with deep grievances against Díaz´ *rurales* and the rich landowners of the north. Villa had been independently fighting federales since Madero´s call to arms was published. Madero was a man of wealth, respected, with a strong family behind him. In his first armed encounter, he had proven his courage in battle. What better leader could they have? As soon as it was evident that the northern rebels were having success, Emiliano Zapata led a rebellion in the southern state of Morelos . LAND AND LIBERTY, his war cry, flashed across the country. The flickering flame Madero had lighted soon became a blazing prairie fire. Like a string of firecrackers, uprisings were set off in Chihuahua, Sonora, Sinaloa, Coahuila, Durango, Tamaulipas, Guerrero, Morelos, Yucatán. "Madero has loosed the tiger", a senator is quoted as saying.

In his journal, a friend of the Maderos, Albert Blair, wrote: "San Antonio, March 17, 1911 - President Taft is amassing thousands of American soldiers along the border from Brownsville to El Paso. Big American ranchers are yelling at their congressmen for protection. American investments in Mexico exceeds more than one billion dollars, more than the capital owned by Mexicans themselves. An Army officer from Fort Sam Houston told me to tell my friends (the Madero boys) that if that mess down in Mexico heats up, one shot across the border and Uncle Sam stops their show´… Three days ago Pancho Villa stormed the city of Torreón, Coahuila, the most important railroad junction in the north and the center of the cotton plantations. The Laredo Times reports that it was a bloodbath. Seems Villa also slaughtered three hundred Chinese, senselessly, shooting up their laundries, pushing them out the windows of their banks and gambling joints, herding them like cattle to the edge of town. Seems they are descendents of the coolies brought over from China by the United States to work on the Union-Pacific railroad who drifted down into Mexico to try their luck. Poor devils. Villa´s a barbarian! But the fact remains, he took Torreón.

March 31 – Got a long letter from Raúl Madero. He´s down the line with Pancho Villa and Francisco. I quote: "Every day raw recruits show up ready to lay down their lives for the Revolution, Mostly they´re fodder for the Federal cannons. No boot camp this, no time for training, but they keep coming. We lose two or three hundred then the army swells again with fresh volunteers looking for a way out of the cornfields. Villa's troops have been fighting federales incessantly since December, with only a bowl of watered down beans in their bellies and a sarape to keep them from freezing at night. You must know that Villa spent sixteen years outrunning and outwitting federales and rurales, Francisco has acquitted him of all crimes and he's one hell of a loyal officer, a shrewd tactician and not a yellow bone in his body. We've got the federales jumping through hoops now. We chase those blue hats, draw them in, pulling them out of garrisons to defend towns we let them take, then take back. Saves ammunition and keeps them off balance. Down here you ride like hell, attack, retreat to the hills, sleep wherever you fall, eat tortillas and beans, get cactus spines in your rump and seldom have a bath. Are you sure you want to fight in this Revolution?"[34]

Several hundred American volunteers joined Madero's Revolution: Guiseppe Garibaldi, grandson of the liberator of Italy, headed a contingent of Texas volunteers, Madero's chief strategist was General Benjamin Viljoen, a veteran of the Boer War and recent New Mexico rancher who trained rough campesinos into his commandos. Pancho Villa's dynamite expert was Oscar Creighton, a former New York stock broker. The best trained soldiers were defectors from the Federal Army.

In late April, gathering forces, gathering strength, Madero turned north to face the Federal garrison in the important border town of Ciudad Juárez The rooftops of

---

34 Source: "In the Shadow of the Angel" by Kathryn Blair

El Paso, Texas, across the river, were crowded with business men looking through binoculars, ladies in flowered skirts holding parasols and opera glasses, workers peering through telescopes - all keenly watching the battle of Juárez raging across the river. The battle of Juárez was decisive. On May 10, 1911, it was over. On May 21, on a table with the headlights of an automobile for light, the surrender agreement was signed. Díaz and his Vice-President resigned. A provisional President would take over pending a new election.

Madero and his entourage took the train to Mexico City where victorious David who had felled Goliath was welcomed by flag-waving crowds and brass bands on every station platform. As his train approached, a terrible earthquake shook Mexico City, an omen that dismissed the old regime, it was said. An omen of disaster, others prophesied. Throngs gathered to welcome him, young boys scampered up buildings to sit in window sills or clambered up on statues to see him. "**Madero y democracia!**" they yelled. The bells of all the churches clanged joyously when he broke out from the crowd and descended from his carriage at the Palace.

Age defeated Díaz as well as the ill-taken decision to be reelected one more time. His Generals were old and their swords rusty. He signed his resignation as President with an excruciating toothache. With his innate generosity, Madero provided Díaz with an armed escort to take him to Veracruz where he sailed for France and exile. Accompanying him were many of his Ministers and elite supporters who preferred exile to living under the new Revolutionary regime. In Veracruz, flowers were strewn in Díaz´s path and the strains of La Golondrina, the Mexican farewell song, brought tears to eyes as the last notes drifted across the water to the Ypiranga sailing for France. Don Porfirio was leaving….

Díaz died in Paris in 1915. The first World War had started and the bloody aftermath of Madero´s Revolution engulfed Mexico, shattering the country and destroying all that Díaz had established. Although many requests were made, Porfirio Díaz´ remains have never been returned to Mexico. His tomb can be seen in a chapel in Montparnasse, Paris.

Two men from Oaxaca dedicated their lives to the integration of Mexico. One saved the Republic, the other united Liberals and Conservatives which made peace and progress possible. In official history books, Benito Juárez is depicted as a hero and Porfirio Díaz as a villain. Both tenaciouisly remained in office – one, vehemently loyal to the law, the other ignoring or bending the law to suit his purposes – both convinced that they acted in the best interest of the country. However they are judged, these two men from Oaxaca are giants in Mexico´s history.

Francisco Madero´s presidency lasted only fifteen months. It is said he was naïve, he was an idealist, he trusted people, he believed in the basic good in man.

He chose to wait to be legally elected, an election he overwhelmingly won in a free, untampered vote. The interim President, León de la Barra, had remained in office six months. A porrfirista, de la Barra considered Madero.s revolution "a gush of passion" which must be contained and its efforts channeled". De la Barra considered himself a disciplinarian in the midst of disorder. He was, in fact, out of his ambience. During his six months in office, he sabotaged Madero´s efforts to find accords, especially pertaining to the one major problem – land reform. Zapata had refused to lay down his arms demanding the immediate return of ancestral lands usurped by rich hacendados. Madero insisted on legal procedures and asked for patience. The killing, sacking and destruction of the haciendas in Morelos had left wounds too deep to heal. The best way to arrive at an agreement was to speak with Zapata personally,

Zapata arranged a meeting with Madero in the town of Cuautla, near Cuernavaca, territory of the Zapatistas. He demonstrated a conciliatory attitude. Without Madero´s knowledge, de la Barra ordered the Federal Army to enter the town and start a violent campaign against the zapatistas. The outcome was evident: Zapata suddenly mistrusted Madero´s motives and cancelled the meeting. He issued a proclamation calling his people to take the land themselves! Fighting federales, burning and looting haciendas, killing hacendados and their families was to continue for years.

Madero guaranteed freedom of the press, permitted trade unions to grow and exercise the right to strike, instituted free breakfasts in the schools, built schools, "A good government can only exist when there are good citizens," he is quoted.. An honest, frank individual, his demise was the result of his trust in people. He kept on many porfiristas in the Congress, left the Federal Army in the hands of one of Díaz´ top generals. After all, was not the Army´s job to serve the nation, to obey its Commander-in-Chief? He was

now Commander-in-Chief. His close friends and supporters, even his astute brother, Gustavo, warned him that he
should get rid of all Díaz´ men, especially the Generals. De
la Barra had disarmed and dismissed Madero´s revolutionary forces, keeping a few experts whom the Federals labeled
"bandits". With optimism and patience, Madero continued
to face his tasks. He firmly believed that true democracy
and respect for the law would bring the nation together.

On Febrary 9, 1913, a plot to permit the escape from
jail of one of Díaz´ top Generals and former Governor
of Nuevo León, Bernardo Reyes, began what were to be
known as "the ten tragic days." Madero had already put
down three rebellions but this was in the city.

Reyes and his followers rode through the city and across
the zócalo to the Palace gates in an attempt to take it – and
were gunned down. Shots were fired in every direction,
killing innocent citizens. Soon after, a barracks uprising
broke out. They were firing in the streets! Felix Díaz, a
nephew of Don Porfirio, had also broken out of jail and
taken the citadel, the arms storehouse! Madero sent General
Victoriano Huerta to put down the rebellion. Instead, the
fighting grew worse. . Bodies were piling up, doused with
kerosene and incinerated. A nauseous stench filled the air…
It was all a carefully planned plot to capture Madero in the
Palace and take him prisoner. .

A more despicable character in Mexican history cannot
be found than General Victoriano Huerta. In an emotional
speech, he pledged loyalty to Madero while plotting to
overthrow him. The day before the Reyes attack, Madero´s
brother and advisor, Gustavo, was tricked by Huerta,
imprisoned and assassinated in a most barbaric manner:

drunken soldiers tortured him, mutilated him and finally shot him.

Another treacherous antagonist was the Ambassador of the United States, Henry Lane Wilson. An arrogant man who considered Madero inept and crazy,[35] a President who was a threat to American property and commercial enterprises, Wilson became a rabid, irrational enemy of the government to which he was accredited. Among his accusations was that Madero would not take his advice. Sought by Huerta, Wilson promised him immediate United States recognition for ousting Madero. Wilson had been sending alarming reports to President Taft and when the rebellion broke out in the streets of Mexico City, he wired Taft that the country had become ungovernable when, in truth, the uprising was local. Ambassador Wilson indicated to the press that Taft would order a military intervention if Madero continued his irresponsible actions. With Madero a prisoner in the Palace, the diplomatic corp and Madero´s family urged Wilson to use his office and influence with Huerta to assure the President´s safety. Wilson´s reply was that he could not interfere in the internal affairs of Mexico.

Madero and his Vice-President, José María Pino Suárez, were removed from the Palace, placed in separate automobiles and driven to the penitentiary where ostensibly, the cars were ambushed by forces that attempted to rescue them and, in the confusion, were accidentally killed. Wilson wired U.S. President Taft that he accepted the explanation and advised American Consuls in Mexico to do the same and submit to the new government. Years later, Madero´s assassin, a military officer, confessed to the murders.

35 Madero was known to have practiced spiritualism.

Before he was taken from the Palace, Huerta had succeeded in forcing Madero to resign his office as President in exchange for clemency for himself and his family. Convinced that his family was in danger, Madero signed. With the resignation in hand, Huerta faced a friendly Congress which acknowledged that in view of the President´s resignation, by law the interim President became the Minister of the Interior, Pedro Lascurain. Mr. Lascuráin´s name is listed among the President´s of Mexico although he lasted in office only forty-five minutes. By previous agreement with Huerta, he named Huerta Minister of the Interior, signed his own resignation as interim President, thus leaving the office open for Huerta. The farse was rapidly executed. Very correct. Very legal.

General Victoriano Huerta was hailed by the old porfiristas, the elite, the landowners and the free press as a hero and the new President of Mexico. Ambassador Wilson could not live up to his promise of immediate recognition of Huerta by the United States Government. Taft did not believe the story of Madero´s death and in two months, the newly elected President, Woodrow Wilson, friendly to Madero, was vehement in his refusal to recognize the Huerta Government as legitimate. The stage was set for the avalanche of protests that led to the Revolution that took the lives of one million Mexicans in the following seven years.

CHAPTER XV

FEBRUARY 18,1913

Governor Venustiano Carranza of the state of Coahuila, looked at the telegram in his hand with mounting fury It was from Victoriano Huerta, advising all Governors that, approved by the Senate, he was now the Provisional President of Mexico. Usurper! Traitor! Carranza called an emergency meeting of the Coahuila State Legislature and obtained a mandate to disavow the legality of Huerta´s presidency. The Constitution did not grant the Senate the right to designate the President of the nation! Carranza lost no time in contacting other northern Governors and leaders, many, friends of Madero - still a prisoner in the Palace. Four days later, news of Madero´s "unfortunate" death caused Carranza to add another word to his diatribe against Huerta. Assassin! The only solution to this intolerable situation was to raise an army and oust the usurper. Legality must be restored! And Madero´s death avenged!

Tall, erect, dignified with a well-combed white beard, Carranza projected confidence – a man of authority who had been appointed Governor by Madero. Resolutely, he called up the small armed groups in Coahuila, professional guardians of the public safety, and armed troops that guarded the countryside. Others joined his armed band thus giving birth to the "Constitutionalist Army." Since he was not a General, rather a man of means and a politician, Carranza declared himself "First Chief of the Constitutionalist Army". The small army soon swelled. In Chihuahua, Pancho Villa committed his support. Outraged by Madero´s assassination, Villa recruited miners, cattlemen, railroad workers, bandits and campesinos who for centuries had endured the tyranny of officials and injustices of the rich. He swept through the border towns, to honky tonk cantinas and red-light districts where a fight was always under way. Whether one fought with the federales or the constitucionalistas made little difference. Fighting was a way of life and booty ones´ reward. Life was cheap. The population of the north ran the gamut between the mainly illiterate work force and enterprising, educated men of culture.

The response to Carranza´s call to join his army was immediate. His cause, to oust Huerta and avenge Madero´s death, also rallied civilians, many from the middle class. His most valuable General was Alvaro Obregón, from southern Sonora. Obregón was a rancher and small business man who had sided with Madero. He was intelligent, charismatic, and proved to be an outstanding military strategist. He passionately shared Carranza´s views. Obregón raised an army in the northwest, General Pablo Gonzalez was placed in charge of the northeast and PanchoVilla the North. In the South, Emiliano Zapata had never put down his arms. "Land and Liberty" was still his battle cry and any cruelty was acceptable to destroy the haciendas and retake the ancestral Indian lands. He, too, joined Carranza´s cause.

Huerta had been President Diaz´ Commanding General and was admired by his troops for his toughness, his cunning and ability as a soldier. He also had the backing of the wealthy porfiristas and the Catholic Church. From the beginning, Carranza knew that for his leadership and cause to succeed, he first had to defeat and disband the *federales* (something Madero had not done). The constitucionalistas would have to fight federales all the way to Mexico City.

> *Villas´s powerful Division del Norte soon took over the railroads. His troop trains rolled by… powerful locomotives belching smoke … coal cars …steaming baggage cars. On top, soldiers, with their legs dangling over the side, held tight to their women under a fiery sun, soldaderas who would light a charcoal fire in some desolate field, who would feed them, nurse them and fire a rifle as well as their man. …Pullmans were crammed with the fortunate – officers - a blur of brown faces. Horsemen churned up dust along the track, Villas´s elite Dorados riding guard in their yellow shirts and Texas hats, more feared than Satan himself. Flatcars bristled with cannon… freight cars with munitions –Howitzer, Louis and Maxim, Winchester… Hospital cars wafted up iodine, staffed with inexperienced practitioners preparing to swab down the wounded day and night. Cattle cars packed with live feed rolled by .. freight cars and more freight cars filled with cotton, thousands of*

bales of booty bound for the market in Mexico City. Last, the caboose with little flowered curtains fluttering at the window, the efforts at housekeeping by Villa´s latest "wife".[36]

Sacking cities, raping, looting, plundering churches became the way of the revolucionarios as they fought their way south. Only General Alvaro Obregón of the Army of the Northwest discouraged these practices. He was known as a disciplinarian, a man with cool wisdom, well-liked by his men. Carranza wanted Obregón to enter the Capital first, pacify the citizens and prepare the way for his own entrance.

In the Palace in Mexico City, Victoriano Huerta assessed his position: President Taft had not recognized his government as Ambassador Henry Lane Wilson had promised. Now, another Wilson, a professor- type, was in office up there and he had clamped an embargo on Huerta´s arms delivery. Woodrow Wilson had made a pact with Villa – arms in exchange for not damaging American properties or interests. Well, Huerta decided, he would negotiate with the Germans. That country was bursting with arms, ready for war. Huerta had dissolved Congress, put all the senators in jail; he had only to sign his own name on a German arms contract to make it legitimate. Huerta´s plan leaked out; President Wilson would not permit Germany to arm that assassin! Ostensibly to prevent German ships from entering the harbor, on April 21, 1914, Wilson ordered the blockade of the port of Veracruz by the United

---

36 Pancho Villa is known to have forced a priest, at gunpoint many times, to marry him to make his current woman "feel good". He neither smoked nor drank.

230

States Navy. American marines occupied the city. In the ensuing battle they killed several hundred civilians and a number of young naval cadets who tried to defend their city. Mexicans were enraged at the invasion and bombardment by the United States. It was a violation against the rights of a sovereign state! Huerta´s defenders bombarded the press: the oil barons in Tampico, Hearst in California and the American cattle ranchers along the border were publishing damning articles about the constitucionalistas wave of destruction. The United States and European investors viewed Huerta as a return to the status quo which had greatly benefited them under Díaz. The same was true of the wealthy class and the Church in Mexico. They all felt that only Huerta could stabilize the country and urged Wilson to raise the arms embargo. Wilson stood firm. He insisted that an institutional government would better serve U.S.-Mexican relations than a military government. Ironically, it was later revealed that the German ship sailed south down the coast and delivered his arms to Huerta. To no avail. After a year and a half of trying to consolidate his position, Huerta knew he was finished – victim of the broken promises of one Wilson and persecuted by another. Woodrow Wilson had gotten France to retract a big loan and England to retract recognition. President Wilson threw his weight behind Carranza. Huerta was trapped: Zapatistas to the south, Constitucionalistas rapidly advancing and the Americans in Veracruz. He chose exile, leaving the next in line interim President in his place. Secretly, Huerta made his way to the port of Coatzacualcos where he embarked for Europe, from there to New York, then made his way to El Paso, Texas, where he hoped to slip across the border and raise another army. Ill, his liver ravaged by alcohol, Huerta was caught, imprisoned in Fort Bliss and a year later died, officially of cirrhosis, poisoned by maderistas, some historians conjecture.

Pancho Villa and Obregón raced for the Capital, fighting bloody battles all the way. Determined to prevent Villa from entering the Capital first, Carranza cut off the coal for his locomotives leaving the road free for Obregón to enter the Capital in his name. On August 15. 1914, Obregón arrived, riding at the head of the Constitutionalist Army. No church bells rang, there were no fireworks nor shouts of "Viva". They were met in silence, observed by mistrusting eyes. The wary citizenry now faced the fact that the Revolution had accomplished the unthinkable – taken and occupied the Capital! Obregón´s first act was to step out on the balcony of the Palace and address the restless crowd that packed the zócalo. "There will be no looting," he stated. "The First Chief of the Constitutionalist Army will be here soon to establish peace and order and restore legality to this nation." His second act was to round up 180 priests who had come to the Capital to escape the Revolution, hold them hostage in the Palace, and demand 500,000 pesos from the Church for their release.

Carranza´s triumphal entry was greeted with flowers and flag-waving. The peace accord was signed and the Federal Army unconditionally surrendered. Unable to face the difficult and complicated situation, the interim President simply left the country. The Revolution was over!

The next armies to arrive were Pancho Villa´s and Zapata´s marching through the city creating terror in eyes that beheld them. The Zapatistas swarmed over the city seeking food, more humble than the villistas., the Virgin of Guadalupe their banner. Villa forcibly took over the big mansions as headquarters for his Generals and men. As a temporary stable for his elite cavalry, Villa commandeered the unfinished Palace of Fine Arts. Following suit, Zapata´s brother took half of the empty Palace as quarters for his men and stables for his horses.

Suddenly, Carranza, Obregón, Villa and Zapata looked at one another. The office of President was empty! Who was the legitimate heir to head the government? Already, rifts among them were strong. Villa did not trust Carranza; he called him "Don Venus", a *perfumado* whose uniform and well-combed white beard were always impeccable. A crafty one, Villa declared. Everyone knew that Carranza wore dark glasses, with his back to the sun, to cast light on his visitor´s face, his own in shadow. He, Pancho Villa, had won this Revolution. Maybe he should try the Presidential chair. (There is a picture proving that he actually sat in it). When questioned about his ambition, with a smile, Villa said, "este rancho es demasiado grande para mi" (this ranch is too big for me). Zapata had no political ambition: he only wanted to overthrow the creoles and capitalistic landowners. Land was life, *mi tierra* was synonymous with home. Zapata´s motto was: "The land belongs to those who work it." Obregón would continue to back Carranza as long as he carried out his intentions of forming a legally constituted Government.

Carranza immediately called for a Convention in which all factions would meet and elect an interim President. After much discussion, the neutral city of Aguascalientes was chosen as the site. Unable to stem the discord, Carranza failed to attend the Convention. He was not elected interim President. The elected President was Eulalio Gutierrez, a General without strong ties to any of the factions. Villa and Zapata walked out, then convoked a Convention of their own. Carranza called for a Convention of his followers which restored his command.

The Revolution had fractured. Villa and Zapata broke with Carranza. Disorder ruled. Between November, 1914 and October, 1915, three separate interim Presidents were named by the *convencionistas* who chose their own convention sites and representatives. Battles now broke out among the three factions: who held the Capital, was temporarily in charge. Like Benito Juárez, Carranza decided to move his headquarters to Veracruz.

Of all the revolutionary leaders, Carranza was the most qualified to govern. He was a shrewd politician who knew how to administer a government and demand respect for authority. He knew that only he could impose peace. He would wait out the infighting among Obregón, Villa and Zapata and see who emerged the winner. In Veracruz, he quickly negotiated an accord with Woodrow Wilson to withdraw his navy from Mexico´s most important port. On November 23, 1914, the United States Navy sailed home. For a year, Carranza spent his time formulating and issuing a series of necessary reforms while battles raged among the factions up in the highlands.

The year of 1915, the citizens of the Capital suffered the ravages of the infighting. The worst ravage was hunger. In their homes, people rattled empty containers: beans, rice, flour, sugar, dried corn, milk cans. All empty. They vied with the dogs for a scrap from the garbage cans. Rage welled up, rage at the warring revolutionaries who had halted the city´s supply wagons and trucks, confiscating their provisions while they fought their bloody battles. Hungry, angry people lashed out in vain at the ever-changing revolutionary forces that rode into the Capital, taking possession, imposing their rules and their money, annulling the authority of the previous faction. Iron curtains slammed down as furious grocers and shop keepers refused to accept their worthless paper money. Hunger, like a vise, had tightened its hold on all but the five hundred Generals the Revolution seemed to have produced.

Bands of soldiers roamed the city, breaking into houses and stores, stealing whatever took their fancy, yanking up floorboards for fuel. Generals careened down the streets in commandeered Daimlers, Italas, Cadillacs, Mercedes, Renaults, Hudsons, smashing fenders at will. In the bars, bullets accompanied the loud verses of "La Cucaracha". Pancho Villa kidnapped a beautiful young French woman, creating an international incident between France and Mexico. He claimed he did not know she was French.

On a small ranchito in the countryside, a young girl pulled at her grandmother's skirt. "I hear horses," she said in a barely audible voice. Her grandmother stoically continued stirring the pot of weeds and a few beans. They were all the same: carrancistas, zapatistas, villistas. They had raided three times, taking her boys, shooting her husband who refused to join them, taking their mule, their pig, their chickens – and finally, her daughter who had left screaming. "There is one baby chick left," the old lady said. "Tie its beak and legs and hide it in the bushes." She looked at her young grandaughter, just turned twelve. "I dug a trench in the chicken coop. Get in it and lie down. I will pull a wooden plank over it and cover it with straw.. Don´t worry. It has breathing holes." The pounding of hoofs was closer now.

Still a loyal *Constitucionalista*, Obregón set out to defeat Villa, the invincible *Centauro* of the north. In one of the bloodiest battles of the revolution, Obregón met Pancho Villa in the city of Zacatecas. Having read all he could on modern warfare, taking place in Europe, Obregon´s barbed wire and trenches mutilated Pancho Villa´s cavalry in their brutal charges. Piles of dead horses of the proud *Division del Norte* slowed Villa´s advance until he was forced to retreat. Later, during the deadly battle of Celaya, Obregon´s right arm was shot off – Pancho Villa´s "revenge". Obregón had obtained a biplane and his Mexican pilot had launched the first aerial bombs in Zacatecas. He now bombed Villa´s retreating army. Battle after battle, Obregón chased Villa north until, totally weakened, he surrendered in Chihuahua and put down his arms.

Carranza returned to the city in August, 1915, threatened by a general strike and faced by a populous that was furious and starving. He moved his headquarters to the village of Guadalupe, away from the turmoil, and began putting in motion the plan he had formulated in Veracruz: In 1916 he invited every state to participate in a Constitutionalist Convention. The Constitution of 1857 no longer covered the necessities of 1916. Overcoming his suspicion that Carranza was negotiating with the Germans, now at war with France and England, in 1915 Woodrow Wilson had put an arms embargo on the sale of arms to Villa and officially recognized Carranza as the interim President, pending elections. The famous book, "The Zimmerman Telegram", by Barbara Tuchman, traces the Germans´ attempt to maneuver Carranza into aggravating the United States to the extent that they would "intervene" to protect their northern Mexican investments, mainly oil. "Intervention" meant troops, troops tied down in Mexico, a war to divert their attention from Germany. Zimmerman was the German Minister in Mexico and when his famous telegram was intercepted and decoded, the plot fanned the anti-German feeling in the United States.

Mexico suffered economic starvation, all commerce with its big European investors was shut down by the war in Europe and much of its border trade was intervened by irregular troops. In 1916, to get even with the United States, which had withdrawn its support from him, Pancho Villa raided Columbus, New Mexico, shooting up the town and killing Americans. Carranza had no recourse but to permit General Pershing to cross the border in what became known as the "Punitive Expedition." to catch and imprison Pancho Villa. A year later, Pershing left, never able to catch his illusive prey. He is quoted as saying "Villa is everywhere and nowhere."

In 1917, in the city of Querétaro, the Constititutionalist Convention met. The defeated villistas and zapatistas were not admitted, but a representative number of delegates from every state attended. The new Constitution dealt with every social, political and economic demand that had given rise to the Revolution. Most important were articles

27 which gave the nation jurisdiction over all its lands and its subsoil, article 123 which dealt with labor relations, article 3 which dealt with education and 130 which defined church-state relationship. The delegates were witnesses to a new, revolutionary state, one which was to cement reform over a long process.

Carranza was elected President by the convention for the period 1917-1920. He was more a patriarchal figure than politician who accepted his role as a Constitutionalist President with firm faith in the law. But reality soon drove him to crude practices. His time in office was plagued by uprisings, hunger, epidemics, strikes. He was not in tune with the new ideology promulgated by the Constitution, especially the "radicals" who defended the laborers´ rights. He did not understand that new generations knocked at the door of government. During his presidency, he made countless mistakes: each caudillo (local chieftain) expected recompense for his role in the Revolution and Carranza permitted them to rule as they pleased, also allowing rampant corruption among his administrators. His years serving under Diaz had given him a certain "play-one-against-the-other" attitude. With his power and authority, he sometimes exercised the limits of cruelty. In 1919, he ordered his most feared General, Pablo Gonzalez, to finish off Zapata. Hounded and pounded by the carrancistas, the zapatistas had retreated, split into bands, no longer an army. Having eluded capture for years, Zapata was caught in a carefully planned act of treachery and shot.

Carranza made his biggest mistake as the Presidential succession approached in 1920. Ignoring the clamor of the majority to support the candidacy of the victorious, popular and charismatic General Álvaro Obregón, Carranza turned his back on Obregón and chose a puppet, an unknown civilian who was Mexico´s Ambassador in Washington. "The Revolution is not the prize of Generals," he stated. "We need a civilian, a man who will uphold the law." The obregonistas loudly reviled him. To compound his problems, the Governor of Sonora accused him of meddling in State affairs. Carranza´s response was to send an armed force north and decree the disappearance of all local offices. The inevitable took place: an armed uprising in Sonora. In short time, rebellions broke out throughout the country., led by caudillos who felt they had not received their due lot. After one month of riots, Carranza stood alone, his dream of controlling the presidency finished. His pragmatic character told him it was best to leave the Capital, move his government again to Veracruz where he could reconsolidate his position as had Benito Juárez.

Taking with him the national treasury, Carranza boarded a train and headed southeast. Betrayed by his former friends, surrounded by enemies, the trip was short. Armed bands ambushed the train. Carranza escaped into the mountains of Puebla with a few loyal followers, including General Rodolfo Herrera.. After days of enduring rain, heat, and hunger, Carranza and his small band came to the village of Tlaxcalantongo. Resigned to his capture, he accepted the hospitality of a campesino and lay down on a straw mat under a thatched roof to sleep, commending his soul to God. At dawn on the 21 of May, 1920, Carranza was assassinated by an armed soldier under the command of General Rodolfo Herrera who declared that Carranza had committed suicide.

Dozens, if not a hundred books have been written about the Mexican Revolution. One million Mexicans were killed, the wealthy country left by Porfirio Diaz destroyed, villages, haciendas, towns ravaged, displacing people from their *tierra* synonymous with home. The scars of the Revolution was left in the hearts of succeeding generations. Considered an agrarian revolution, not a political one as in the case of the Bolshevik, it lasted for ten years – 1910-1920. Commenced by Madero whose banner cry was "Effective suffrage, no re-election", after his tragic, treacherous assassination, it remained "Land and Liberty" for Zapata, and a legitimate reason on the part of the Constitutionalists to oust Huerta and restore a legal, elected government. But the Revolution never really amalgamated; soldiers were loyal to their local *cacique* who was, in truth, defending his own interests. After Huerta was defeated, the Revolution broke into three factions which waged a civil war for nearly three years. History demonstrates that it is impossible to stop a Revolution. It must run its course. With the election of Carranza as the Constitutional President, it should have concluded. But the residues – revenge, resentment, inconformity, lust for power - were still smoldering. There was no true winner. Madero, Carranza, Zapata, Villa, even Obregón were all assassinated. Yet out of the blood bath there arose a new spirit of nation. The Constitution of 1917 guaranteed national sovereignty over its lands, its subsoil, its natural resources, dealt with agrarian reform, education and workers´ rights. To cement a firm, democratic, well-grounded new state, under new laws, was the challenge of the future.

CHAPTER XVI

While Carranza was fleeing, a Revolutionary army took over the Capital and installed an interim President, Adolfo de la Huerta, a close collaborator of Obregón. Fortunately for Obregón, who was soon duly elected by Congress, de la Huerta had concentrated his efforts in establishing peace in the torn nation leaving a smoother path to the Palace when Obregón took office at the end of 1920. The term had reverted to four years with no re-election.

Alvaro Obregón was an authoritative, practical man of action. As Carranza´s Secretary of War, he had established a medical school for the military, a Department of Aviation and a munitions factory. He was wise enough to realize that his military merits could not sustain his administrative responsibilities. The wealthy conservatives, the Church and the United States government considered him a radical. Ignoring their admonitions, he felt he must tackle the still unresolved social problems first. Education was a must.

Many intellectuals and professionals who had left in self-exile began to return to Mexico. Among them was José Vasconcelos. Obregón named him Secretary of Education.

Never in Mexico´s history has the government allocated so much money to education. Twenty percent of the Federal Budget was designated to teach the lower classes to read and write.

Illiteracy surpassed 85% of the population. Vasconcelos was a writer and philosopher, a highly educated man who had taught in Universities in the United States and Europe. He organized a modern crusade: his teams of "teacher-missionaries" went out to remote towns and villages to build schools and train teachers. If you taught people to read, they had to have books. As a young boy, Vasconcelos had lived in a border town and crossed the bridge every day to attend the American school on the other side. He read every book in the library of that small school. Each of the schools Vasconcelos opened in Mexico had a library. His thesis was "a book is a portable school". The first impulse to create an editorial industry had been launched.

With equal fervor, Vasconcelos instigated a cultural revival. He joined with a group of intellectuals to form the *Ateneo de la Juventud*, a literary society for youth. After ten years of revolution, the young writers and poets were eager to enter the modern world, to express new ideas. Mexico was twenty-five years behind Europe and the United States. At the petition of Diego Rivera, Vasconcelos met with a group of painters, among them José Clemente Orozco, Fermín Revueltas, Robero Montenegro and David Álfaro Siqueiros – and offered them walls to paint on. The venerable old colonial buildings downtown were soon alive with color where painters straddled scaffolds to paint their own gospel of the Revolution. The name Lenin made headlines about another Revolution; fur hats made their appearance on the university campus. Diego Rivera professed his belief in communism and joined the party.

Antonio Rivas Mercado, former Director of San Carlos, the School of Art and Architecture, who had been responsible for granting Diego a scholarship to study art in Paris as a young student, looked up at the mural Diego was painting on the ceiling of the Preparatory School. Disproportionate, heavyset women looked down from different angles. A voluptuous nude blonde in the curve of the dome made the Professor shudder. Diego called down. "This one represents wisdom. What do you think, maestro?" "If she is wisdom, then I pray that the ignorant inherit the world!" Pulling the brim of his hat down, the professor walked away.[37]

Most important, during Obregon´s tenure, labor came under the patronage of government. Early on, labor leaders had sought the backing of government in their demands for higher wages from foreign employers, especially in the oil and mining industries. Mexicans were paid a minimum amount while foreign workers earned high salaries. Now, a powerful labor leader, Luis Morones, flexed his muscles. An unwritten pact between labor and government was in the making. Obregón conceded the right to strike exclusively

---

37 Antonio Rivas Mercado had been the Director of the Academy of San Carlos which had granted Diego Rivera his first scholarship. (From "In the Shadow of the Angel" by Kathryn Blair.

to Morones´ union. He instituted Sunday as a day off with pay. To further secure the support of labor, Obregón offered lucrative posts to its leaders, incorporating them into the state-run apparatus. The "bought" votes of the labor unions was a basic support during the long regime of the PRI. Today, they still enjoy impunity and render accounts to no one.

Although land distribution was not carried out rapidly, Obregón´s grants of small parcels for ejidos did establish an alliance between government and the rural population which, in years to come, brought the peasant population under the total domination of the government. One of Porfirio Díaz´s adages was "give a dog a bone and he will stop barking"

A thorn in Obregón´s side was the fact that following Carranza´s murder, President Woodrow Wilson of the United States had not recognized the legality of his government as had most of the nations of the world. The foreign investors who owned oil production, railroads, mines, electricity and banks were openly hostile. Irregular armed forces were still raiding and labor was pressing for higher wages. Obregón chose to court the United States: he used his influence over the Supreme Court to concede that the Texas Oil Company´s contract preceded article 27 of the Constitution and thus it had rights over the subsoil. New perforations doubled the oil production. Obregón also agreed to pay an enormous debt to the United States which immediately led to an agreement of friendship and commerce. In 1923 a trainload of new equipment and technology arrived in Mexico. The American business men and engineers were entertained in the castle and the

Treaty of Bucareli, was signed[38] During Obregón´s term the Constitution was amended to allow a second term after an interim presidency. In 1924, Plutarco Elías Calles took office. The agreement was that Calles would turn over the government to Obregón again in 1928.

Calles was a revolutionary General chosen by Obregón. He was a strong leader and good administrator, more political than military. Obregón had assured the alliance of labor and government, now Calles concentrated on constructing an economic basis that would help the country to grow. He founded the Bank of Mexico, extending credit to the incipient national industries. He also founded the Rural Bank to boost agriculture. He opened schools in working class neighborhoods, accenting sports and practical courses. During Calles´ term, irrigation schemes were explored and hundreds of miles of highway were built. Soon, cities were buzzing with "fotingos" (inexpensive Fords) bringing families closer together. Rural Mexico began to change to an urban population.

Calles´ was the founder of the party which was to become the PRI. He "institutionalized" the Revolution.

In 1927, Dwight Morrow, a member of J.P. Morgan, was sent to Mexico as Ambassador from the United States. Most past Ambassadors had treated Mexicans as inferiors and had shown little respect for Mexico´s rights as a sovereign power. Instead of remaining aloof or threatening, Morrow immediately sought friendship with Calles. To flatter the Mexican people, Morrow invited Colonel Charles Lind-

---

38 In official history books, this treaty was considered a nefarious act on the part of Obregon.

bergh to make a good-will visit. Lindbergh´s solo flight across the Atlantic in 1927 had established him as an international hero. It was at the American Embassy in Mexico City that Lindbergh met his future wife, the Ambassadors´ daughter, Anne Morrow. And it was Dwight Morrow who commissioned and personally paid Diego Rivera to paint his famous murals in Cortes´ Palace in Cuernavaca. With genuine affection for Mexico, the Morrows had bought a house in Cuernavaca and spent most week-ends there.

The threat of rotation between Calles and Obregón caused uprisings that led to violence and assassinations. Politicians of every persuasion wanted to share the power. It was a well-known fact, that obregonistas as well as callistas were amassing fortunes. It is said that Morrow convinced Calles of the importance of institutionalizing the Revolution – turn Revolution into Institution, give it substance, meaning, use it to legitimize his Presidency and future administrations. In 1929 the PNR (Partido Nacional Revolucionario) party was born. It adopted the national colors and became instantly linked to the State. Later, its name was changed to PRI (Partido Revolucionario Institucional). The ruling clique became sole heirs to the political and economic future of Mexico for the next seventy-one years. Mock elections were held every six years to simulate a democracy.

The most important challenge Calles faced was the Catholic Church. Having suffered extreme desecration of its temples and degradation of its priests during the Revolution, the Church had lost control of education, cultural and political influence, all now constitutionally accorded to the government. In 1926, the tension reached a head-on collision. Calles closed the churches and sent the priests and nuns into exile. From 1926-1929 the cry of "Viva Cristo Rey" (long live Christ the King) rang across the mountains and valleys of the western central states of Mexico – centered in Jalisco, Guanajuato and Michoacán. Ranchers felt the agrarian reform was more a threat than a solution and joined the guerrillas. The wealthy Catholics in the Capital formed the National League for the Defense of Religious Liberty and helped arm rural guerrilla groups. Many families hid priests in their houses and carried on religious rites there. The *Cristeros* never had a unified army but were hard-core fighters. Calles knew that the real base of his power was the army. He increased the size of the armed forces keeping the Federal Army happy with pay-offs and privileges. Instability must be stemmed at all cost. In 1929, peace with the *Cristeros* was finally achieved, brokered by the United States with Ambassador Morrow instigator of the agreement. The Government promised not to invoke all the anti-clerical laws in the Constitution of 1917, and the Church agreed to stay out of politics. In 1928, just prior to this peace agreement, Alvaro Obregón had been pronounced the official candidate of the PNR party.

A shockwave was soon to shake Mexico. On July 17, 1928, at a luncheon in his honor, a Catholic fanatic drew close to Obregón and shot him point blank. Constitution-ally, Calles could not succeed himself. He categorically refused to extend his term or run again in the future. In his speech to the nation, he announced that any legally constituted party could convoke a congress to elect and propose a candidate. Quickly assembling a PNR congress,

Calles proposed General Portes Gil as the interim President, pending a general election in 1929. To allay fears of perpetuating the rule of obregonistas, Calles again amended the Constitution to declare the presidential term six years without reelection. It has remained thus ever since.

José Vasconcelos, the charismatic Secretary of Education under Obregón, was sought by a group of intellectuals and politicians to run as the candidate of Madero´s old Anti-Reelection party. He campaigned throughout the country, forming political clubs, giving speeches in bull rings and plazas in small towns and cities, preaching his unquestionable belief in equal justice, opportunity – and above all, education. He promised to do away with corruption and fight for equal wages between Mexican and foreign workers. In the campaign of 1929, Vasconcelos also offered women the right to vote.[39]

As the PNR candidate, Calles pushed through then Ambassador to Brazil, Ortiz Rubio. An unknown in Mexico, he was a perfect puppet. When Calles realized that Vasconcelos was gaining force and might win, the party machine went to work: vasconcelista leaders began to "disappear", meetings were boycotted, lights turned off in the plazas where Vasconcelos was speaking, and finally, in plain daylight, Germán de Campo, one of Vasconcelos young orators, was machine gunned in the presence of a crowd of witnesses in Mexico City. The day of the election, the city appeared to be under siege: certain voting centers mysteriously remained locked, boxes of votes disappeared, bullets rang out throughout the day. When it was over, Ortiz Rubio was officially declared the winner by two mil-

39 Mexican women obtained the right to vote in 1953.

lion votes. Vasconcelos was allotted 12,000. So went the first election under the PNR.

Ortiz Rubio resigned after two years. The general belief was that his family had begged him to resign after an assassination attempt. Those who read the fine print learned that, daring to flex his presidential muscles, he had fired two of Calles´ appointees. The next day, he read in the paper, "Due to bad health, President Rubio has resigned." General Abelardo Rodriguez completed the term that ended in 1934. A local joke told to tourists by taxi drivers was: "This is where the President lives", pointing to the castle – "but that is where his boss lives", pointing to a house near the park. These six years were known as "El Maximato" and Calles was "el jefe máximo."

From 1934-1940, Lázaro Cárdenas, another General and protégée of Calles, became one of Mexico´s strongest, most controversial and beloved leaders. He declared he was a socialist, not a marxist. Like Calles, he was anticlerical, favoring a socialist education in which religion was never mentioned. He declared liberty of religious faiths, encouraging the protestants to return...Some historians call him the last revolutionary statesman. After his government, the social and political promises of the Revolution were forgotten. Cárdenas traveled the length and breadth of the country to see for himself the true needs of the poor. An authentic socialist, his land reforms were sweeping. He confiscated the large haciendas and ranches as well as tracks of land inherited or held as investments, including land owned by foreign companies. Some extremists, held aloft the hammer and sickle.

Young Mariana had just finished her breakfast when she heard a distant clatter of horses coming up the long, tree-lined road to the hacienda. Who had her parents invited? In the kitchen, discussing lunch with the cook, Mariana´s mother also heard the clatter. She looked puzzled. A young stable boy came bounding through the central patio of the house bumping into Mariana. "Son muchos," he said, breathing hard. "Revolucionarios!" Mother, daughter, servants ran outside, soon to be joined by the "Patrón". Mariana´s father had a fleeting memory of "Villistas" galloping up to his father´s ranch. He knew who these horsemen were - the radical henchmen of the local government authorized to issue an expropriation decree. In a cloud of dust the brigade of horsemen pulled in their reins. The standard they carried was the hammer and sickle. Mariana watched the leader jump down from his horse and hand her father a paper. "Your hacienda has been expropriated," he announced. He looked at his watch. "You have thirty minutes to gather your possessions and leave the premises."

During his tenure, Cárdenas gave 180,000 ejidos, parcels of land, to campesinos, covering 46 million hectars. The Rural Bank made loans to farmers. To counterbalance the growing power of the established labor leaders, he created the Confederación Nacional de Campesinos (national confederation of peasant farmers)

Energy was another of Cárdenas´ concerns: enormous dams were built to light villages and create more irrigated land, especially in the dry north. The city of Monterrey was fast becoming an industrial center. In the cultural world, radicalism was the order of the day: Diego Rivera, David Alfaro Siqueiros and Clemente Orozco continued to preach communism in their murals but on the University campus, professors preferred to keep the socialists at a distance. Liberty of expression was their belief. In religious matters, Cárdenas did not oppose faith in a religion, rather the fanaticism which led to exploitation of the people.

Like Calles, Cárdenas´ greatest challenge was how to deal with the entrenched foreign investors once and for all. Oil had become black gold for the foreigners. For centuries, the native Mexican had collected oil from puddles which mysteriously seeped through the earth. They found it burned and used it in their ceremonies. Under Spain, it was used to calk ships and the Laws of the Indies declared oil the exclusive property of the Spanish Crown. At the beginning of the twentieth century, a Texan, Edward Doheny, struck a gusher in Tampico. The British were fast on his heels. Porfirio Díaz did not levy taxes on oil and the foreign oil companies were granted full rights of exploration. Mexican oil became the source of immense wealth. As Admiral of the Royal Navy, Winston Churchill, had converted the British navy from coal to oil, encouraging Mexican exploration by the British petroleum investors. The first World War proved the superior efficiency of oil over coal.

In 1936, a general strike broke out paralyzing oil production. The Mexican oil workers demanded a raise in salary and better working conditions which were privileges enjoyed only by their foreign fellow workers. The oil companies howled in protest, declaring they could not afford to meet the demands. The situation festered. To prove that Mexico was Captain of its own ship of State, and that control over its natural resources was its constitutional right, in 1938, Cardenas expropriated the American and British oil companies. Shouts, accusations and threats went up, but he remained firm. After feverish and useless negotiations, the foreign oil companies dismantled their plants, refineries and oil ducts, removed all infrastructure, maps, plans, diagrams and manuals. The sale of tankers was denied. The expropriated companies organized a boycott of Mexican oil. The British Government raised such an angry protest that Cárdenas broke off relations. President Roosevelt, on the other hand, recognized Mexico´s right to expropriate the foreign companies, asking only for fair compensation. Cárdenas was forced to deal with Germany, Italy and Japan – oil for machinery – on the eve of the second World War. The Treasury was almost empty. Negotiations about compensation continued for several years until finally the Shell Oil Company and Standard Oil of New Jersey reached an agreement with the Mexican Government. The people of Mexico vociferously supported the expropriation, even the Church. "Expropriation Day", November 20, is a national holiday. Petroleos Mexicanos had to start from scratch. Pemex, as it is called, is still government owned and subsidized. Calles had set the stage for government control of the economy: now, Cárdenas removed all outside sources of power and made government funding the central factor in the economy. He granted the labor leaders important roles in the new administration of the petroleum company, and their power has grown ever since. Pemex became and is the number one source of income for the Federal Government.

Cardenas´ humanism made him sympathetic to political refugees. In 1937 he opened the doors of Mexico to exiles from different parts of the world. León Trotsky was a close ally of Lenin, but when Stalin came to power, he was sent into exile, persecuted by assassination attempts and ejected from one European country after another. Diego Rivera pleaded with Cárdenas to permit Trotsky to live in Mexico. Cárdenas agreed. Despite the furor his decision created, Trotsky arrived in Mexico and led a fairly quiet life until his assassination by a Spanish stalinist in 1940. In 1939, Cárdenas welcomed thousands of Spanish Republicans who sought exile in Mexico in the wake of General Franco´s success in the Spanish Civil War. The right-wing Mexicans shouted, "Now a communist wave has washed up on our shores." The Republicanos brought with them the gold of Spain, but where it went is still unknown. Many Spanish intellectuals, scientists, business men and artisan exiles contributed much to Mexico in future years. They were granted Mexican citizenship.

During the first few years of Cárdenas term, Calles had constantly tried to regain his position as Jefe Máximo". To avoid Calles´ continuous appearance on the scene, Cárdenas had him arrested, put on an airplane and flown to Texas and exile. Calles stated to the press: "If the President has ordered my exile, I will comply." Calles´ supporters villified Cárdenas for deporting the man who had put him in power. From Texas, Calles settled in California. An interesting note in the American press of those years was a meeting between Calles and José Vasconcelos, also living in exile in California. Years later, Calles returned to Mexico and died in his house.

In the violent, fraudulent election which followed Cárdenas´ term, the party machinery went to work again. The last legitimate opposition candidate, popular General Juan Andreu Almazán, was politically annihilated. Cárdenas´ choice, General Avila Camacho, was elected for the term 1940-1946.

The election of 1939 set the stage for the future Presidents of Mexico. As the Presidential term was coming to a close, the President selected his successor. His chosen successor became known as "El Tapado" the candidate under the lid. Speculation always brought hurried political alliances around the suspected chosen candidate – who was not always the one under the lid, a secret divulged at the last minute when the party convened to "elect" its candidate. Those who had made the wrong overtures and alliances, were known as *quemados*, the burned ones who could not expect prize positions in the next administration.

During these World War years, the agrarian reform all but withered as the economy took precedence. Mexico signed a commercial treaty with the United States in which it was to supply all its internal production of strategic war materials - oil, minerals and heavy fiber in exchange for credit to modernize the country. A stable internal Mexico also meant a stable border, an important factor for the United States. Early in the war, the brasero program was born; thousands of Mexican field and factory workers flooded across the border – legally – with a renewable work contract. It should be noted that a steady stream of illegals also crossed. Roosevelt named the new relationship the "Good Neighbor Policy." At the end of the war, it was evident that economically and politically each country,

Mexico and the United States, had to take its neighbor into consideration. As Mexican exports vitally increased, new oil wells gushed their black gold, roads and railroads expanded. The Banco Rural continued making loans to farmers with corrupt administrators raking off a substantial personal gain..

Farmer Nacho Perez drove his brand new, shiny tractor right up to his compadre's small adobe hut. "Here it is, compadre. The Banco Rural is letting me make payments. I sold my oxen. This machine will plow the fields in a few days, then we plant, then it will harvest a huge crop of onions and we will be rich! Nacho's compadre gazed at the tractor. "You have put all your profit in that machine... what happens if it doesn't rain?"

CHAPTER XVII

As the golden years of the Second World War ended, so, too, did the rule of the Generals. Carranza, Obregón, Calles, Cárdenas and Avila Camacho had never pretended to embrace the rules of democracy.[40] A radical change in the political direction took place with the election of Miguel Alemán, a lawyer, in 1946. Henceforth, the long rule of *abogados* (lawyers) commenced.

1946-1952- Alemán quickly discovered that there was a large world out there starting a process of reconstruction after six years of war. Charismatic, energetic, eager to put Mexico on the international map, he began traveling abroad. Aware that foreign investment was necessary for the growth of Mexico, Alemán broke with the "revolutionary group" and used his charm to foment an expanding economy with a view to industrialization. He presented

40 The descendents of those generals are today among the wealthy elite of Mexico.

Mexico as a new "democratic" nation eager to participate in the post-war world. The population in Mexico had doubled since 1930 and a growing middle class demanded the Government´s attention.

During his tenure, Alemán began to modernize Mexico City – new buildings, new avenues, parks, he donated a large tract of land to the National University and created a sprawling, attractive campus with a stadium for "futbol", Mexico´s favorite sport. He cleaned up Acapulco, turning this beautiful, natural harbor into a favorite jet-set playground and in the process becoming a millionaire. The mordida (bite) became the key to doing business and corruption filtered down through all levels of government. Yachts from around the world were seen in Acapulco´s harbor during the sixties and seventies – Acapulco´s glamour days.[41]

1952-1958 – Ruiz Cortinez is best remembered for granting the vote to women.

1958-1964 - Among the PRI Presidents, Adolfo Lopez Mateos stands out. He had been a young *vasconcelista*. From 1958 to 1964 a new, golden era developed under his administration. Mexico´s "Special Relation" with the United States continued, magnified by European investments. Economic growth had engendered a more cosmopo. litan, urban society which made a good income from new, small businesses. Lopez Mateos created the Social Security Institute. He fomented free and accessible education. The

---

41 Today, Acapulco is a holiday resort for the Mexican middle-class. A new super highway has shortened the driving time to little over four hours from Mexico City.

government issued free text books, albeit written from the revolutionist point of view: Porfirio Díaz was depicted as a malevolent dictator and Zapata and Pancho Villa were heroes. Among Lopez Mateos´s legacies was the construction of the National Museum of Anthropology, considered one of the great museums of the world.

With the advent of Fidel Castro on the Latin American scene in 1959, Lopez Mateos succeeded in maintaining a balance between the conservatives and pro-Castro liberals for the duration of his term. Under Lopez Mateos, the government bought out the foreign energy interests. The Light and Power Company, created by Porfirio Díaz, was still owned by the British and Canadians. Growing state control brought loud protests from the industrialists, especially since labor strikes were upheld by the government. Labor flexed its muscles more and more. In the private sector, an emerging generation of technocrats was forcing the government to look beyond its self-serving bureaucracy.

The Bay of Pigs fiasco fanned strong anti-American demonstrations all over Mexico. On the university campus, the strong leftist wave surged with placards and banners and T-shirts of their new bearded idol and martyr, Che Guevara. The Cold War had created a wide chasm between the left and the right. The leftist movement was affecting much of Latin America. Mexico had escaped the endemic military coups in the southern hemisphere thanks to the PRI´s control of the army and a stable economy. Riots and protests were rapidly put down by the army with the usual roster of unexplained disappearances. To counteract the growing leftist effect on Mexico, Lopez Mateos chose a conservative, pro-American to succeed him.

1964-1970 - Gustavo Díaz Ordáz is best remembered as the President who permitted the massacre of students in 1968. A student uprising in France was the incendiary torch that led to other student uprisings in other countries. Government control of the preparatory schools in Mexico stifled free expression and spurred a riot among the young students. Soldiers occupied the preparatory school campus and student leaders were arrested. University students were quick to support their cause and uprisings in defiance of the government began to swell as thousands of marchers headed in the direction of the zócalo and the National Palace. Mexico City was in the throes of frantic efforts to complete the last details of its preparations for the Olympic Games scheduled to open in October. An investment of $80,000,000 was at stake and news of the student riots was spreading. Soldiers soon occupied the university campus. After two months of continuous student clashes with the police and army, in his address to the nation on September 1st. President Diaz Ordaz vowed that nothing would prevent the opening of the Olympics on October 12. On October 2, nine days before the Olympic flame was to be lit in the University stadium, student leaders called for a massive meeting in Tlaltelolco, properly named the Plaza of the Three Cultures to commemorate the last Aztec battle where *Cuauhtemoc* surrendered to Cortes. Hundreds of students and civilians congregated in the afternoon. Their purpose was to retake the campus of the nearby preparatory school occupied by the army. Suddenly a cordon of police circled the plaza backed by armed soldiers. When student leaders refused to be pushed out, the soldiers fired into the crowd. Hundreds of students and civilians (it is claimed) were gunned down or arrested. Bodies were quickly dragged off. To this day the massacre of Tlaltelolco is still unresolved, still on the agenda of the courts, families still demanding to know what became of their children or relatives. Many may have died in prison, not listed in the prison lists. When true stories began to surface, it shocked Mexicans and the world.[42]

The word "Tlaltelolco" became deeply rooted in the collective conscience of the Mexicans. Many writers and political analysts consider "Tlaltelolco" the end of an era. The PRI had shown its inability to deal with new, independent-minded actors on the stage. Dialogue was not in their vocabulary. The Government denied all fault and put a clamp on the press. Analysts reason that it should have been the moment to remove the mask of "democracy", bury the banner of the Revolution, reform corruption-ridden Pemex and begin the real process of education where the student was taught to reason, not memorize. It was the moment to face the real problems of poverty. It was the moment to reassess the role of government. To paraphrase Enrique Krauze (internationally known historian, writer and political analyst): "To simulate democracy had become second nature. El teatro (play) had become real. The mask had fused with the face." The farce of democracy that the PRI presented had been running for years. The actors had control over the tickets and bought the critics in advance. Freedom of the press was a line pronounced on the stage. A special comedy played in towns and villages every six years: the audience was trucked from one town to another to ap-

---

42 The Olympic Games opened on schedule and Mexico was applauded as a magnificent host in world opinion.

plaud the local candidate and rally a few more "supporters" in the town plaza. A lunch box, high sounding promises and, when necessary, a bribe provided compensation. The PRI threw a few bones and a seat or two in Congress to the only legitimate opposition – the PAN, National Action Party. The massacre at Tlaltelolco should have closed the theater. But "the mask had fused with the face".

At the end of this post-war, stable economic period, ten percent of the population received almost half the national income, the richer northern states being first in line. Rural Mexico had become semi-industralized Mexico. It had increased in population, the poor growing poorer, resigned to Papá Gobierno´s hollow promises and sporadic provision of health clinics, wells and more land. The illiteracy rate was now 70% of the population and the daily wage about five dollars a week.

1970-1972 - The two presidential periods of Luis Echeverria and José Lopez Portillo stand out as black pages in the history of the PRI. Their twelve years in office are known as "La Docena Trágica", the tragic dozen, a play on words of the "Decena Trágica", the ten tragic days of uprisings and treachery which led to Madero´s assassination. During their terms inflation was rampant. The government printed money to give the illusion of wealth. The dollar, pegged at $12.50 for the past twenty-two years suddenly jumped to $20.00 in 1976 and kept rising. It is to be said in his favor that Echeverria´s public investment in health care and education were a priority during his time in office.

In 1973 Echeverría declared Mexico a third world country and hosted a Third World Congress. The word "anti-imperialism" was decried in the university among political groups, labor unions and the intellectual left. The United States was the "imperialist" bad man who could be blamed for most of Mexicó´s ills. When the Organization of American States broke relations with Cuba and expelled Castro, Mexico abstained from voting and has maintained relations with Cuba all along. A shout went up when Echeverria gave one third of the grounds of the Conservatory of Music in Mexico City to Cuba for its Embassy. After the fall of leftist President Salvador Allende, in Chile, Echeverría welcomed thousands of political refugees from Chile as well as from military regimes in South America. Mexico was a paradise.

The discovery of enormous new oil deposits in the southwest was a saving grace. Oil prices went from 3.00 dollars in 1970 to a high of 35.00 dollars per barrel in the next few years. Oil saved Echeverría´s administration from total economic disaster. When Lopez Portillo took office in 1976, he bragged that every Mexican would share in the oil boom. Suddenly, in 1981, the price of oil tumbled and interest rates on the public debt rose. The Government was forced to cut lavish spending. Lopez Portillo declared that he would defend the peso "like a dog". The peso jumped from 26 to 70 to the dollar, daily losing value. Inflation was near 100%. Dollar accounts were frozen.creating an uproar.. Mexicans awakened to headlines that President Lopez Portillo had "nationalized" the banks. Salaries fell and unemployment rose. Vendors took to the streets, crowding the downtown area, occupying plazas and sidewalks. Thousands upon thousands began to cross into the U.S. illegally. Many of Mexico´s professional class either secured jobs or emigrated in search of work. The PRI looked on as the corrupt police force demanded higher and higher bribes or defected to rising drug dealers.

Toward the end of his term, Lopez Portillo built a huge family complex of lavish houses (his own, a mansion) for himself and his family on top of a hill within Mexico City. The complex was on government property, supposedly a green reserve. Mexicans, in their ironic humor related to politics, named it "El Cerro del Perro", the hill of the dog.

The financial crisis of 1982 began to augment the fissures in the political system and focused the attention of the financial world on Mexico. If Mexico declared a moratorium on its external debt, it would rebound in the international markets. The image of an unstable, corrupt Mexico began to appear in the press. Surging immigration and drug traffic worried the United States. President Clinton looked for a way to help Mexico avoid a financial crisis and renegotiated the debt. He did not put pressure on the terms of payment. The pressure was on Mexico´s inability to deal with the drug traffickers and the growing problem of illegal immigration. Corruption in the police force and throughout the government had peaked. Still, the PRI looked on. Passing his problems on to his successor - so as not to be held responsible – was the modus vivendi of the President at the end of his six year term.

1982-1988 -Miguel de la Madrid, who followed Lopez Portillo, received a country in economic and moral ruin. "Moral renovation of society" had been his campaign slogan. An economist with a Master´s degree from Harvard, he believed that a more efficient system would make the embedded bribe more difficult to hide and help the economy. First the terrible corruption in the police force and abuse of authority, permitted by Lopez Portillo, had to be faced. De la Madrid arrested the police chief and put the former director of Pemex in jail. Public sentiment suggested putting Lopez Portillo on the carpet to restore faith in the Presidency. The "Imperial President", as Enrique Krauze has named the Presidents of the PRI, was immune and untouchable as was the rest of the royal family, Secretaries and Congress. They remained in hibernation during De la Madrid´s tenure. The speeches on Revolution Day sounded hollow. Modern Mexico was awake. A terrible explosion of a gas duct which killed dozens and demolished a large area brought to light the lack of maintenance of Pemex. The union, too, was untouchable. In 1985, a powerful earthquake destroyed a large part of downtown Mexico City. President De la Madrid was slow in taking action let alone efficient measures. His first statement was, "We do not need outside help. We will handle our catastrophe ourselves." The citizens took the matter in hand: with rapid and spontaneous action, rich and poor, young and old formed civic groups and rescue teams went to work. Nobody waited for "Papa Gobierno". "Papa Gobierno" was rapidly dying. To increase De la Madrid´s headaches, Cuauhtemoc Cárdenas, son of Lázaro, defected from the PRI to form a new left-wing party, the Partido Revolucionario Democrático, the PRD. Other left-leaning and "burned" priistas defected with him giving political substance to the new party.

De la Madrid chose a young technocrat, Carlos Salinas, a Harvard economist, to succeed him. Protests were vehemently shouted by the old guard but in short order quieted down. Deference to the President was the law of the PRI. Cuauhtemoc Cárdenas campaigned vigorously and was favored by some pollsters as the potential winner. Unlike other elections when the public seldom bothered to vote, this time lines of voters waited for the voting booths to open. New computers were installed to count the vote. By afternoon it looked like Cárdenas was winning. Suddenly it was announced that the computer system had "crashed". The next morning de la Madrid declared Carlos Salinas the winner. The party machine was still working.

1988-1994 - The advent of Carlos Salinas in 1988 brought a new focus to the economy and Mexico´s world view. With the fall of the Berlin wall in 1989, the Eastern European block of socialist countries also fell. The utopian soviet state, born with the Russian Revolution of 1917, imploded. Marxism had unequivocally failed, and with it, socialism.

Recognizing the vacuum left when Mexico severed relations with the Church, Salinas put through a measure to reestablish relations with the Vatican. On the third visit of popular Pope John Paul III to wild acclaim in Mexico, Salinas officially welcomed the Pontiff with the decorum afforded by his office. Formerly, by decree, the President was not allowed to attend church or church functions in any official capacity.[43]

Salinas was ready to reform the entire economic system

43   When President and Mrs. Kennedy (Catholics) visited Mexico in 1962, President Lopez Mateos was not able to accompany them to a special mass at the Basilica De Guadalupe in their honor.

and went into high gear. An intelligent young man and an adroit manipulator, he used his position as President to push through his ideas, often by Presidential decree. The word neoliberalism entered the vocabulary. A new market reform was imperative. Salinas put many state owned companies, including the banks, on the international auction block. He defied the unions by putting Pemex´s most powerful and corrupt union leader, "la Quina", in jail. Addressing the ever fermenting question of poverty, he changed the Constitution to allow the *ejidatarios* to own their land. Until then, the land could be used by the peasant family in perpetuity as long as the land was worked, but the campesino had no deed and his *ejido* became an insufficient tract of land to support a growing family. Salinas paved village roads, built thousands of kilometers of new roads, built hundreds of schools and hospitals, dug wells for potable water and brought electricity to rural communities. He put an end to the never-ending, sacred and never resolved agrarian reform which had been continually used more as an instrument of control than a solution to the problem. It had permitted seizure of great tracts of land, including land belonging to foreign companies, and corruption was common practice. Secretary of the Agrarian Reform was eliminated from the President´s roster during Salina´s term.

Although loyal to the PRI, Salinas had a new outlook on governing. Looking north, Salinas feverishly worked for a free trade agreement with the United States and Canada, his personal crusade. It would eliminate trade tariffs between the three countries and closely link the northern hemisphere. After heated debates, the Free Trade Agreement was finally ratified by the United States Congress in 1993.

In 1996, Mexico joined the World Trade Organization opening its markets to international trade. Salinas publicly boasted that Mexico was now a first world country. A new pride in Mexico and the President´s achievements spread through the population.

During Salinas´ term, inflation continued to rise reaching catastrophic rates. By Presidential decree, Salinas removed three zeros from the peso-dollar exchange rate. The poor market vendors suddenly felt poorer; they were accustomed to dealing with paper bills in denominations of one hundred, five hundred and even a thousand pesos for their vegetables, fruit, meats and flowers; now a few coins were exchanged for their goods. Their thousands in paper money were, in fact, almost worthless. Money fled from the country as investments and accounts were withdrawn. Salinas´ hopes for a stable economy had ricocheted, his first world was in economic chaos again.

Casting a shadow of accusation on Salinas personally were the assassinations of his choice for successor, Donaldo Colossio, killed on the campaign trail. Soon after, Salinas´ former brother-in-law and prominent member of the party, José Ruiz Massieu, was assassinated, shot at point blank in his automobile. Salinas´ brother, Raúl, was accused of drug involvement with millions deposited in a Swiss bank. To compound this ignoble end to his tenure, shortly before his term ended, a guerrilla group rose in Chiapas, headed by masked Subcomandante Marcos, thought to be a professor from a university in Mexico City. Calling themselves the Zaptista Army, television showed masked and armed guerrillas threatening the government. On that note, Salinas chose a moderate successor to step into his quagmire. After fruitless attempts to clear his name, not long after retiring from office, Carlos Salinas left Mexico to eventually live in Ireland.

In 1994, Mexico was a country in bankruptcy with an urban society subjected to robbery, homicides and kidnapping. The drug dealers were beginning to penetrate the schools. Ten years of economic instability had seen the increased encroachment of shacks blanketing the mountainsides surrounding Mexico City, testimony to the twenty million inhabitants that make up the population of the Capital and environs. Heavy traffic clogged streets and highways, Drug traffickers were also penetrating the border. The Free Trade Agreement had not brought the expected bonanza to rural Mexico, nor had it created the expected number of jobs. The land, much of it eroded from decades of poor farming methods, was not even producing enough corn for the indispensable tortilla. Truckloads of cheap, subsidized corn from the United States made even modern farming incapable of defraying the cost of production. Many of the farms lay unattended as fathers and sons chose to cross the border illegally in search of work to support their families. This was the panorama when Ernesto Zedillo took office in 1994.

1994-2000 - Ernesto Zedillo was a pragmatic man who had not been in line for the presidency. He had headed the campaign for the assassinated "chosen one", Donaldo Colosio, and had seen Mexico´s problems up close. In spite of the fact that he was handed an economic crisis, Mexicans began to see a head of State who was ruling in the interests of the nation.. As his term came to a close, Zedillo knew the time had come for the vote of the people to be respected. The "dinosaurs" were furious, there were dozens of fraudulent tricks he could have used. As he viewed the longest line of voters in Mexican history, Zedillo waited until the polls closed and the count was tabulated. Looking directly into the television camera, the last PRI President in the line of succession announced that Vicente Fox, the opposition candidate of the PAN, the National Action Party, had won by a fair margin.

Ernesto Zedillo is regarded as President of the transition to real democracy. For seventy-one years, the PRI´s electoral machine had operated on its own perpetual dynamic, naming Governors, Municipal Presidents, Congressmen and Senators. Congress was the rubber stamp of the President; the Legislative branch servant to the Executive. The Revolutionary Family was first in the hierarchy. Those in favor with the President were guaranteed a lucrative position in Government. They could go from Cabinet position to Ambassador of a top country to Governor of a State .It was likened to the central authority of the Aztec Tlatoani and the Spanish Viceroy upon which Mexico laid its roots. The one-party PRI system was described by writer Mario Vargas Llosa as "the perfect dictatorship."

The year 2000 ended the reign of the "Imperial Presidents".

CONCLUSIONS

It is agreed by most Mexicans that for all its faults, the PRI made one major contribution to the nation: for seventy-one years it maintained the peace, creating stability. The PRI protected big business, left the Church alone, controlled labor and the rural population. Uprisings were quickly put down; peace by force guaranteed stability and Mexicans were ready for a reprieve from revolutions. During its long regime, the PRI built schools, highways, Social Security hospitals and clinics. Village roads were repaired and new ones built to connect the country, communications continually improved and illiteracy fell to about 15%. Still, today the poor represent fifty percent of the population. Basic problems still fester.

Looking back, there are infinite "Could haves" and "Should haves" The PRI is blamed for not attacking the drug cartels. With the control it wielded it could have suppressed their growth. It should have implemented quality education instead of catering to the Teachers Union. It could have passed legislation to help curb corruption in government and the police. The vital importance of dealing with the "untouchable" Pemex union should have been addressed. Money invested in rural improvement might have kept immigrants at home. But self-serving .party loyalty came ahead of national interest. There was no long-term planning: the PRI never looked beyond the six-year term. Corruption threaded its way through every government office and through the civilian population – a collusion which satisfied both. One could buy one´s way out of most situations. An old joke defined the rule of law as a flexible stick that could be bent, twisted, broken and discarded when necessary. The attitude of the average citizen put his personal interest above the law. If it wasn´t convenient, why comply.

The year 2000 marks the first democratic change of government in Mexico´s history. Vicente Fox, candidate of the PAN – National Action Party – was freely elected President. Although he has been loudly denounced for infinite misjudgments and oversights, he introduced, and Congress passed, some new rules of governing: All government officials must reveal their economic worth when they take office and State to Municipal governments must render accounts for how their allocated budgets are spent. The throttle on the press has been released. The public has access to government documents. Transparency and dialogue are new words in the government´s vocabulary. Most important, Fox maintained monetary stability during his term. Citizens awakened from their lethargy.

During the current regime of Felipe Calderón, also

a member of the PAN elected in 2006, some necessary changes have passed by majority vote but many more have been blocked. Shouts of "Fraud" by the the party of the left - the PRD - still echo over the election of President Calderón. Much criticism has been thrown by opposition parties on the shoulders of Presidents Vicente Fox and Felipe Calderón but transparency and dialogue are advances that cannot be denied and Congress, with its multiple new parties, is learning to debate issues.

Mexicans still have little trust in government To be elected a politician is judged to be the fastest road to riches. They know that cronyism is the party´s glue. But a new attitude is emerging: with TV, internet, blogs and the like, people are well informed and seeking information on their own. Instead of shrugging off a problem with the usual "Así es" (that´s the way it is), many are saying "Hasta Aquí" (enough!).

Mexicans have lived through crisis throughout their history. Without trust or belief in government or the law, Mexicans enclose themselves in their homes. They look upon the latest national crisis with a certain laissez-faire – "this too, will pass." It is the family that provides stability for Mexico. The family takes in the jobless cousin, the old maiden aunt, the widow, the single mother. Grandmothers take care of the children of working mothers. Women are the axis of the family. With the flow of immigrants that cross the border, today more than ever, women are in charge. And it is not just women in the villages and on the farm. City women, educated women, women in the business world, women in every walk of life are joining or forming civic groups to find solutions to local problems.

The Mexican woman has thrown off her cloak of martyr-dom and has found a voice. Community unity and self-reliance is being encouraged, especially in the indigenous communities where, with the help of organized womens´ associations, markets for beautiful native crafts are being opened around the world, creating direct income for the rural family. European tourists, especially, are finding their way into rural Mexico.

Mexico has so much to offer: beautiful beaches on three seas: the Gulf, the Caribbean and the Pacific - pyramids and ancient sites throughout the central and southern states - charming Spanish colonial cities spread through the central highland which enjoy a year-round temperate climate, No other country in Latin American offers such a variety of regional food, music, dress, dance, customs and crafts. Add the growing industrial sector and private enterprise support for rural education and you have a na-tion on the move.

In his book, "Distant Neighbors", Alan Riding stated: "Probably nowhere in the world do two countries as dif-ferent as Mexico and the United States live side by side … Probably nowhere in the world do two neighbors under-stand each other so little."

Today, with all the positive things that are happening, a black cloud hangs over the border. - the battles and violence of the drug cartels. These cartels find Mexico the shortest route to the world´s biggest drug market, the United States, and with their entrenchment in Mexico, are developing a growing market here. A flow of US arms that cross the border into Mexico are used by cartels to defend their territory with unmitigated violence and license to kill indiscriminately. Armed drug dealers are inching their way into the United States. It will take the full cooperation of the United States and Mexico – a joint responsibility - to win this battle. The bottom line must be to work together as partners. For too long Americans have considered Mexicans incompetent, untrustworthy neighbors and Mexicans have looked at Americans as unjust opportunists who are only interested in exacting advantages. Today, each needs the full cooperation and trust of the other. This also applies to finding solutions to the unresolved immigration problem.

Benito Juárez rose out of the cornfield to become the most important figure in Mexico´s history - the President who believed in and practiced the rule of law, the Zapotec Indian who rose through education, the incorruptible, the avid defender of the Constitution. He is an icon, a beam of light. Mexicans need to believe in themselves, to throw off those deeply buried traces in their psyche of distrust and defeat. If Mexicans work together, if citizens make their voice heard, if those who govern remain steadfast on the new, democratic course the government has taken, with work and persistence a New Fire will forge the great nation Mexico can be – the leader in Latin America.

In 1824 when the Republic of Mexico was founded, it was named
ESTADOS *UNIDOS* MEXICANOS

Kathryn Skidmore Blair
Mexico City, 2011

ACKNOWLEDGMENTS

I would like to thank all those authors who spent all those years compiling all those books on Mexican history that I have read since I was a young girl.

I recommend a few especially interesting books in this collection for readers who might also enjoy them: "Heart of Jade" by Salvador de Madariaga – "The Aztecs" Nigel Davies –"View of the Vanquished" by Miguel León-Portillo, "Quetzalcoatl" by José Lopez Portillo (a former President of Mexico), "The True History of the Conquest of New Spain" by Bernal Díaz del Castillo who fought with Cortés. " The Phantom Crown" by Bertita Harding, "Mexico in Revolution" by Vicente Blasco Ibañez, "My Life in Mexico", by Madame Calderón de la Barca (the Scottish wife of the first Spanish Ambassador after Independence), "Idols Behind Altars" by Anita Brenner, "The Imperial Presidents" by Enrique Krauze, and, of course, "In the Shadow of the Angel" my own book, a family story of the first three decades of the 20th Century in Mexico.

My heartfelt thanks to my much loved friend, Rosita Petrovich, whose Spanish translation is outstanding. My special thanks also to Guadalupe Jimenez, my friend and internationally sought expert on Mexican history who did me the favor of reading the manuscript. I beg her forgiveness for glossing over numerous of the historical "facts" which academics have found to be untrue.

I take sole credit for any mistakes you may find or comments you may not agree with.

Kathryn S. Blair
2011